222 Says
It Was Always You

ROBBY AND MIA GRAHAM

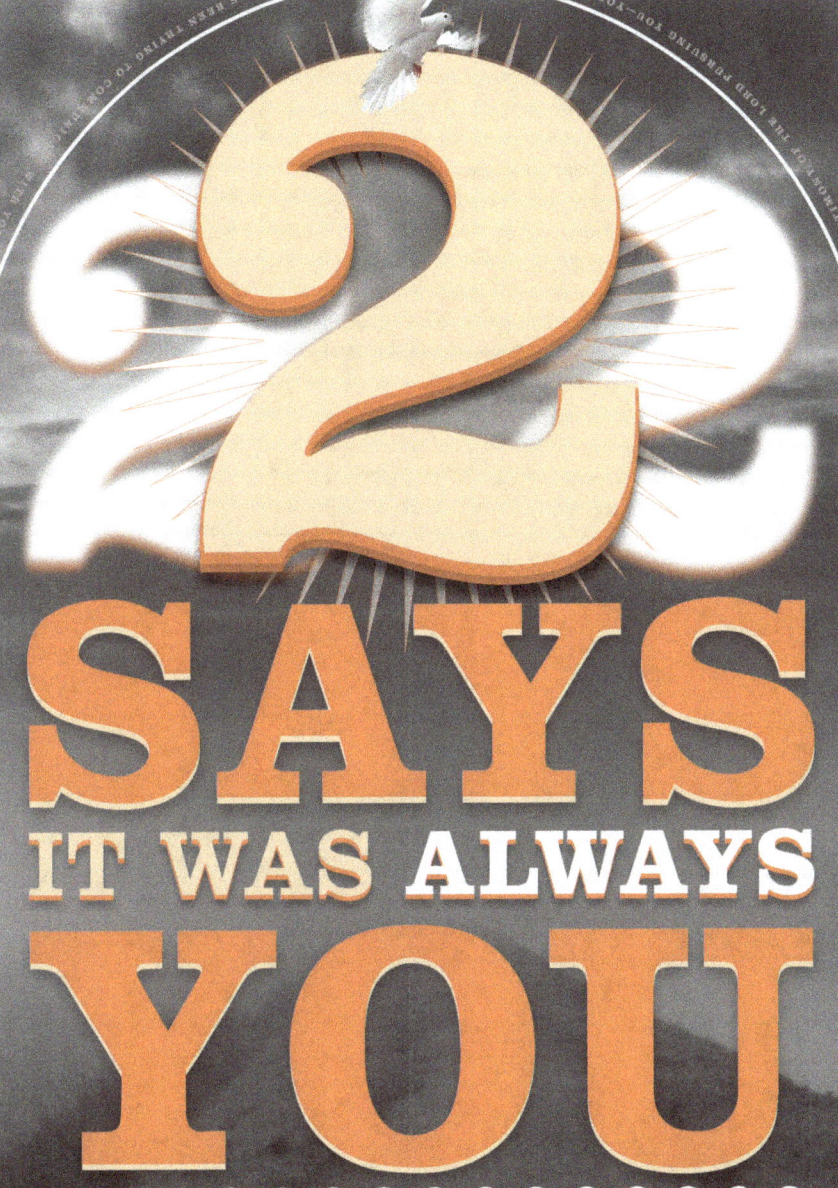

2 SAYS IT WAS ALWAYS YOU

ROBBY & MIA GRAHAM

222 Says It Was Always You
Robby and Mia Graham

Dedicated to the Author and Finisher of our Faith, Jesus Christ!

Acknowledgments

Mia:
· · · · · · · ·

I want to thank *Jesus* for dying to demonstrate God's glory. . .and so that I could live; the Person of the *Holy Spirit*—I do not want to spend even one day without You!; and my *Heavenly Father* for knitting me into my mother's womb with a perfect plan and purpose for my life. I live to bring glory and honor to Your name! Your kingdom come, Your will be done, on earth as it is in heaven!

I also want to thank:

* *Robby* for being my best friend and soulmate—we truly are better together
* My *family* for introducing me to Jesus as a child
* My sons *Blake* and *Ashton* for seeing in me what I could not see in myself, unconditionally loving me through the times when I felt most unlovable, and showing me true grace, mercy, and forgiveness
* *Every intercessor* who prayed for me up to this point and beyond
* And *every man and woman of God* who has sown kingdom seeds into my life

Robby:
· · · · · · · ·

For saving a wretch like me, I dedicate this book to my *Lord* and *Savior Jesus Christ*, my *Father in heaven*, and the Person of the *Holy Spirit* who guides my life every waking moment.

And I want to honor *Mia*, my beautiful wife in these amazing adventures with God; she is a true gift from heaven's most divine.

My appreciation is also to:

* *The Salvation Army Adult Rehabilitation Program*—especially *Majors Paul and Dawn McFarland, Majors David and Pat Waite, Majors Nancy and Stanley Lants, and Major Marilyn White*—for cultivating an atmosphere of healing and deliverance
* *Tampa Christian Fellowship, Grace Family Church*, and *Carl Dobrowolski* of Goodwill Rights Management for believing in us

- My brother *Mac* and sister-in-law *Elsie* for never losing hope in my recovery
- My dear friends *Dale Dudeck, Blake Twedt, Gene Re',* and *Bobby Livernois* for intervening with my addiction, making it possible for me to get the help I needed
- *Blake* and *Ashton* (my two incredible stepsons) for accepting me into their lives
- Their father *Martin* who has been a major, positive influence through this journey
- *John Corry* for seeing God's vision and producing our documentary *Revelations Café*
- All the *characters* in our book and film for their love and support
- *Paige Collins* from Icon Media Group for opening God's kingdom doors
- And last but certainly not least, our "Holy Ghost Writer" *Scott Bueling* for helping us complete God's story

I

"The End"

Robby

• • • • • • • •

April 15, 2013 was another unwelcome Tax Day for many Americans, but for me it was much worse. Being jobless, homeless, penniless, and heavily addicted to opiates, I stood looking in a bathroom mirror, facing the final days of my life. During those wee hours of the morning, as I was coming down from another extreme high—just one more of way, way too many—the lost man looking back at me had become barely recognizable. I stood there welcoming my last breath. Just wanting it over. I was done. With only memories of once having hope, I fell to my knees and cried out to God:

"Cure me or take me out! I can no longer live this way."

Weeping from deep-felt, self-centered sorrow, I fell asleep and woke hours later to the cloudy realization of my situation—total depravity. With withdrawals hitting hard and no money to get more pills, on an impulse I phoned a friend of thirty years, a guy who knew me well and would surely disbelieve what I was about to tell him. Sobbing uncontrollably, I pleaded for Dale to understand why I must die. He had to be wondering who this depraved stranger was that replaced his previously healthy, vibrant friend. I imagined he would hang up in disbelief or at least from wanting nothing to do with this once-decent guy who had apparently thrown his life away. Instead, I heard his godly, confident reassurance:

"Don't do anything stupid. I love you and help is on the way!"

Soon I got a call from Blake, a mutual friend Dale reached out to after listening to me. Now on the board of directors at the Salvation Army Corps, Blake found Christ and turned his life over to God's will, all of which happened while I was spiraling down, completely out of control. Just a few years prior, I had often partied with him, but this day he was calling to help pick up the pieces of my broken life. Blake had me come to his house—where he looked me in the eye and lovingly offered some version of this ultimatum:

"I can help, but only if you promise to do rehab the way you are told to by the Salvation Army Adult Rehabilitation Center (ARC). Otherwise, no deal."

Extremely sick from heavy withdrawals, I committed to Blake's terms. The next day on my mother's birthday, I began the road to recovery. This involved checking into Graham House, a short-time detox facility at the Agency for Community Treatment Services (ACTS), a branch of the Tampa Salvation Army. Graham is also my last name, and later you will learn how the Bible's Book of Acts plays a prominent role in this story. As you will see, only God can script such a string of extreme "coincidences." In fact, the Hebrew language of Jesus's day had no word for *happenstance*—which I take to mean there is no such thing.

After a week, I had detoxed enough to transfer from the Salvation Army's Graham House at ACTS to their ARC treatment facility, where I was expected to spend six months as a full-time resident. First though, a three-day transitional phase had me still taking out-patient treatment at ACTS while temporarily staying at the Amethyst Respite Center. There I was given a small sleeping spot on a rock-hard cot in a room with fifteen other men. This was raw humanity with no privacy, and for an educated man who had previously earned a six-figure income, the reality of bunking with more than a dozen homeless men hit me like a freight train. Amethyst was a crossroads where I would either be humbled and grateful, or return to my self-prescribed medication that would help numb my pathetic last days embracing death.

But I survived Amethyst Respite Center, after which they moved me to cozy, beachside accommodations at a luxurious bed and breakfast— not! Actually, the Salvation Army's finest facilities are their Adult Rehabilitation Centers, so while no boutique B&B, my ARC home was clean and comfortable. They even gave me vouchers to grab some second-hand clothes at a local Salvation Army Thrift Store. However, due to overbooking, my first few nights were spent on a blowup mattress in the library; having escaped that granite cot at Amethyst, this rubber sleeping place felt like a fine hotel's king-sized bed. ARC's food was also better and the overall environment faintly felt like hope, something I hadn't experienced in quite a while as all my life's previous aspirations were flying out the window on the road to destruction.

ARC's room and board were earned through brutal work on the thrift store's docks where they take in donated household items. At age fifty-one I hadn't worked out in six months, I was malnourished, and the opiate withdrawals were still hitting hard. Add to that the 85-degree temperatures of late April in Florida. It's a wet, blistering heat that persists into shady areas because sub-tropical humidity carries the punishing sauna of moisture to wherever you may be; that is, unless you are in air-conditioning—we were not. So imagine heat pounding down on a physically wrecked, somewhat-aged, sickly man who is being asked to spend whole days lifting heavy chairs, tables, televisions, dressers, bed frames, and couches. Was this what desperate people must do? I didn't know but I had made a promise to Blake, and anything else felt like it would lead to my end.

It was a Saturday when I started the job, and my first eight hours working that sticky-hot loading dock felt like an eternity, though we got two brief breathers of fifteen minutes each and a thirty-minute lunch. Without those breaks I would not have survived. In fact, later my exhausted body shut down so completely that I was in bed by 8 pm, something previously unthinkable for this weekend partier. But I was truly grateful to even be alive, let alone experiencing my thirteenth day clean and sober. Though the exhaustion had my head spinning, it would pale in comparison to the next morning's encounter.

Those who reach Sunday while living under the Salvation Army's hospitality *will* attend church, so that April 28th I woke at 7 am, achy and unprepared for radical transformation. When John Newton's immensely popular hymn from 1779 began, "Amazing Grace" immediately brought the impoverished crowd to their feet. It struck me that so many homeless men knew all the words. But as the various-pitched voices rose from their seats, I fell to my knees—sobbing— something I had *never* done before. I broke. This was followed by a feeling of being wrapped tightly in some soft, warm covering, and this was no thrift-shop blanket. I instantly understood my Savior's embrace. Every prior, dismissive, disrespectful thought of Jesus washed away, as a lifetime of lies I had heard about Christ were suddenly circumcised from my heart, making room for the Holy Ghost to move in.

That's all I can explain about the feeling that day, but even looking back now it makes me weep. Having heard some of what a wretch I was, maybe you get how grateful I must have been that morning when Christ graciously welcomed repentance from a completely undeserving failure. This was only days after I had resolved to end up as another uninspired life, whimpering out of existence in some unimaginative and pathetic way, just as the similarly dispositioned devil desires.

What core childhood lessons led me to this point? Though raised in a loving home with two wonderful parents, church was not our routine.

But towards the end of their lives, I believe my parents had grown to love Jesus, judging from them recommending a prominent television preacher. Other than brief lessons leading up to my baptism at age twelve, church wasn't part of my life. I knew of Jesus but had never read the Bible, so I had no clue of what Scripture said about Him. And I did not care because I had life "figured out" at a young age, *feeling* like Jesus was maybe some awesome dude—but no deity—and the Bible was just more of man's ideas, not God's. Being wise in my own mind, I wrongly felt this question I came up with crushed any Christian narrative:

"How could we mere mortals believe a supernatural Supreme Being would need humans to write books like the Bible for Him?"

With that greatly deceived background, imagine me completely transformed during one song! Of course more led up to those life-changing moments when the eyes of a homeless dockworker were opened and I received an unexplainable peace, but it's too much to include here.

Over the next few months, God continued radically changing me from the inside out; I hungered and thirsted for His truth, becoming on fire for Jesus. The more I leaned into Him, the closer He drew to me. Blake gave me David Jeremiah's book *God Loves You,* and after that one I read *Destined to Reign* from Joseph Prince. Both helped me discover who—and Whose—I am. Daily Bible study helped free me from a lifelong drive to gather whatever the world had to offer, liberating me from that shallow self-focus.

The next six months of rehab became all about discovering what God's character is like, who He says we humans are, and what He wants us to do for His kingdom. As a heavenly Potter molding clay, Christ steadily reshaped my thinking toward a desire to glorify Him, living only for the Lord, and selflessly carrying out His will for my life. As for my juvenile question about whether God needs human writing instruments to put out books, just as Jesus enlightened doubting Thomas in John 20, the Lord pointed out that *I* am human and *He* is not. Our Heavenly Father is a spirit, unlike Jesus who is fully man and fully God at the same time.

But the Father does not need a body because He can use anyone to write anything He desires. I would later learn firsthand that the Holy Spirit is able to easily control a person's pen or typing, something He eventually did through me, inspiring the words I would write to the woman He chose for me. This was one of the developments I believe God destined for me, even before my creation. Those initial days exploring God's mind were pleasantly shocking as I began to fathom what my new life might turn out to be, especially being only weeks removed from a depraved existence with no hope. And I cringed when beginning to understand how I had been only days or even hours away from leaving this world for an eternal future of demons, fire, and agony.

Incredibly sold out for Jesus, I began sharing His story with all who would listen, even promising the Lord that I would forgo dating—something I had not done since my early teen years—to be solely dedicated to a life lived for Him. Though never desiring children, I was now making this marriage pledge to Jesus:

> "Lord, if you want me to be with someone again someday, I trust you to pick her out, and if that special person has children, I promise to love them as my own."

By July 3rd I had been in the program about three months when my friend Gene Re' called. Dale and Blake got me into the Salvation Army, but it wasn't long Gene found out and immediately wanted to help as well. We had always been there for each other since age fourteen, and here he was again, helping his brother out. A call from Gene was appropriate because he had been providing me with a phone while at ARC, but the subject of this call was unexpected. When I picked up, at first Gene was reluctant to mention why he'd contacted me that day, and then finally confessed that Michelle from Atlanta was trying to find me. At the sound of her name, my heart raced and spirit sunk, anticipating a conversation with the one who got away eight years prior—but a potentially serious roadblock to rehab. I had imagined I would never hear from her again. Rightly worrying that a re-emerged Michelle might trigger my relapse, Gene reluctantly asked whether he should pass along my information. Though his concern was valid, I was a changed person. Completely surrendered to Jesus.

I asked Gene to have her contact me, she did, and we ended up spending a couple days catching up, something so out of the blue that it seemed God must be bringing her to me for a future attempt at getting back together. But I resolved to do dating His way this time—not the world's. The two days passed quickly and she had to head home to Georgia, but it felt like we might rekindle the old romance. We said our goodbyes with her acting like we would see more of each other. But then she disappeared. No more Michelle. Just gone.

This disappointment made me turn even more to Jesus for guidance and understanding. Why would He bring her back into my life after so many years, only to pluck her away without explanation? At that time, I had not yet discovered Isaiah 55:8–9, an invitation to those thirsty like me, verses where the Lord puts His ways into perspective:

"For my thoughts are not your thoughts, neither are your ways my ways. As *the heavens are higher than the earth, so are my ways higher than your ways and my thoughts than your thoughts."*

Though I was not biblically wise enough to know it yet, God had taken my hand and was asking me to trust Him; the explanations would become apparent over time.

Halfway through the Salvation Army's Adult Rehabilitation Program (ARP), at three months clean and sober I was at peace from fully loving and surrendering to the Creator of the universe, the Savior of my soul. Because I had gotten so passionate to know and trust the Holy Spirit's guidance toward all truth and righteousness, I struggled to attend one of the mandatory Bible studies because the teacher was not walking out what he was talking about. I truly love this individual so I was not judging him, but just needed to stay away from any hypocritical influence. Through other study of Scripture, I would later learn that Jesus too had a problem with hypocrites, and strongly vocalized it to their faces—Christ is no snowflake. Though He's a Lamb. And the coming Lion!

Soon that Bible-class situation would cause another monumental change in my life: getting a bit bold, I asked the resident manager if I could use that Scripture time elsewhere. He thought for a minute and rightly replied:

"Robby, you know I can't bend the rules for you and no one else. If I do it for you, I have to do it for everyone!"

Though sure of getting a second "no," I persisted by offering an alternative gathering that he could credit as a Bible study, which was jumping on the Salvation Army bus with other guys headed to an AA (Alcoholics Anonymous) meeting. They do incorporate Scripture. It may have been the Holy Spirit that suddenly softened his thinking, but either way he just shrugged his shoulders and relented:

"Go on, get out of here. But don't tell anyone about this."

I agreed to remain silent but his change of heart had me suspecting God might be up to something with this meeting. In the *natural* world we see— as opposed to the unseen, supernatural, spiritual realm that permeates everything around us—ARC's necessarily strict recovery program would not have let me on that bus. But this is where the story started becoming less about *me* and more about *we*, a God-glorifying journey of signs, miracles, and wonders in the life of this newly obedient servant.

2

"Okay God, What's on Your Mind?"

So, there I was stepping off a Salvation Army bus at the local AA meeting where I would be attending with a half dozen fellow "beneficiaries," the name given to those fortunate enough to take up six-month residency in the ARC program. Among the benefits is having volunteer alumni drive current participants to places like AA meetings. Graduates often want to pay forward the help they received. In fact, divine destiny would later have me as one of those drivers, but not until getting my driver's license back. It was taken by the state for unpaid traffic violations, and I failed to renew insurance for a car titled in my name, something Florida frowns upon. Praise God Blake allowed me to keep my 2001 Chevy Cavalier parked in his garage while in rehab. Restoring my ability to *legally* drive would take an unknown, huge amount of future earnings, so you can imagine how that thought weighed heavily during my days of addiction and continued through rehab. But at some point there would be restoration, which ended up testifying to God's redemptive power. More on that later.

What's truly unfortunate—but will come as no surprise—is how those traffic violations came from poor decisions made while being high. Some were from me allowing others to use my car for opiate runs, "friends" who disregarded local traffic lights that have built-in police cameras. License plate photos of my car running red signals meant tickets were eventually issued in my name and sent to my last known address. Being isolated in rehab for months, I wasn't around to receive a few of them. The Chevy Cavalier photographed by the police was all I had left, a car inherited after both my parents passed away. It was functional to get me around when not being used for drug delivery, but a far cry from my previous vehicle collection that included a Corvette, convertible 350Z, a custom-built Harley Davidson motorcycle, and an expensive, luxury WaveRunner for my water toy. So, you can see how far my depravity made me fall.

Getting back to the AA meeting, a volunteer who apparently had a license kindly dropped us off there on the evening of July 26th, exactly three months since I had entered the ARC program. Our large group walked in and grabbed some seats, at which time I revisited an earlier conversation with God, knowing He had me there for a reason and would be faithful to answer my question:

"Lord, why this meeting? What am I to hear? Or see?"

By this point in my walk with the Lord, I knew enough Scripture to rely on Jesus's Sermon on the Mount (Matthew 5 through 7) that includes Christians being told to knock on Christ's door and ask for (or seek out) anything *in His name* and it will be granted. As I was asking Him, the chairperson welcomed everyone and disclosed the night's topic: spiraling out of control with alcoholism after having lost a father, mother, or both. There it was. I thought:

"That's why I'm here, Lord! The description fits me. Thank you, God."

My earthly father passed just hours after Christmas dinner in 2007 and because his birthday followed on January 6th, that day we held a celebration of his life (instead of the usual sober ceremony mourning a death). Interestingly, after my recent radical conversion, the Lord revealed how that celebration of dad was part of God's divine plan: January 6th is when the Greek Orthodox celebrate Christ's birthday, as opposed to December 25th when Christians do; if we acknowledge that the Greeks may be right, my father was born on Christ's Greek Orthodox birthday and went home to the Lord on His Christian birthday.

My mother was born on April 16th of 1927, a day that Easter fell on three times during her life, and though we weren't Catholic, she mentioned how she and the larger-than-life pope of the early 2000s (Benedict XVI) were the same age—to the day. That may seem irrelevant, but in the bigger picture I'll paint of God's signs, miracles, and wonders, many less likely "coincidences" going forward will help even the most skeptical recognize the beauty of God's divine tapestry.

While my mother was in hospice care, exactly two years after we held the celebration of my father's life, she passed quietly on dad's birthday. My mom was born during the Easter season when we celebrate Christ's resurrection, and then died on what the Greeks recognize as the day of Christ's birth. After my much-older brother Mac's birth in 1947, the doctors diagnosed her with endometriosis and said she would have no more children—but fourteen years later she had me on July 4th, 1961. God waited almost one and a half decades to unexpectedly bring me into the world—but did so with fireworks on Independence Day. Mac's May 27th birthday sometimes falls on Memorial Day, and to avoid being drafted into the Vietnam War, he enlisted in the Air Force. My father was a World War II combat-wounded veteran. These somewhat interesting correlations are just a warmup of what God, the author and finisher (perfecter) of our Christian faith, had planned for *our* story—His, mine, and another's.

Getting back to the AA meeting, when I heard the talk would be about parental loss leading to addiction, it instantly brought back those memories. But this time God was involved, tying it all into my new relationship with Him, reconciling and comforting me over prior anguish about their deaths. And as mentioned, I wondered whether God meant me to benefit from others talking about the grief of their parents passing, but now I was feeling even more peace about them, and it had already been a while since being severely restless and irritable over losing them.

At that moment I began thinking God might have more in mind for this meeting. Then something out of this world happened: an opening door caused me to glance right, where two ladies were walking in five minutes late—and one looked like Michelle! I thought, *Really, God?* After bringing her back into my newly sober life and me feeling like we reconnected, the one who got away did so again, heading back to Atlanta and completely disappearing. But now You would have her show up at this meeting that I should *not* be at in the first place? Is this how You direct our lives? Wow! Something I will never forget followed those thoughts; in my ear, the Lord quietly and clearly declared:

"That's the one."

I immediately responded:

"WHAT!?!"

Sitting straight up in my seat, any voices in the room began to sound like Charlie Brown's garbled teacher: waa, waa, waaa, waaa, waa, waa. Then as the late-arriving lady got closer, I realized she was *not* Michelle. I don't know whether I was more disappointed or relieved, but this person could pass for her identical twin. The resemblance was hard to believe. Apparently now that I knew she was not the one who got away, the Lord repeated His announcement:

"That's the one."

My head was spinning for the next forty-five minutes of that meeting. I heard nothing spoken in the room because I had an intense dialogue going on between me and my Heavenly Father. Here I was a homeless man just three months clean and sober, seemingly having an argument with my new spirit friend I had committed to serve, *the* glorious Creator of the universe. A few times during the conversation, I peeked around people to take another look at the girl God was apparently going to give me. My future wife. The one. Really!? You would think I was back doing drugs. I had much to tell the Lord, some of which were reminders, as if He needed me to help Him remember what we talked about a few weeks prior. The internal and heated discussion went something like this:

"Seriously, Lord? Why would you point this person out to me when three weeks ago you brought Michelle back into my life, only to remove her a couple days later? You'll remember it caused me to surrender that part of my life to You, telling You I no longer wanted anyone but You, and from that moment forward all I wanted was to do your will, not mine!

"Yes, I did tell You a few days ago that, in the future, if You had someone for me, I would trust You to put her in my life. I also conceded that I had led a selfish existence, not wanting to have children of my own, and that if the woman you choose for me has children, I would love them as my own.

"But with this crucial rehab process and after recent turmoil over the disappearing ex, who I thought I might marry, at this delicate moment You can't really be declaring the woman across the room to be the one?! I am a new creation of just three months, and you know the ARC program frowns on relationships for the first year of sobriety. So, as much as I love You Lord— and believe You're always correct—this does not seem right!"

I then felt a sort of "knowing" inside, something reassuring me that God cannot lie. Looking back, I believe it was the Holy Spirit confirming the Lord's biblical pledge that the Spirit would guide us into truth and righteousness. I thought:

"It must be true. She is the one! According to God."

I then presented this logic to the Lord, after which He was finally able to get another word into the "conversation":

"Lord, I don't have anything to give her. You know I've lost everything and I'm homeless."

Clearly and tenderly, He answered:

"My son, give her your heart."

Depending on your biblical knowledge, all this interaction with God may sound crazy, but Scripture tells us He talked audibly to many people. And like me, other bold souls of shaky faith also argued with the Almighty. Moses was a perfect example: God told him to go confront the ruler of Egypt but being a stutterer Moses *let God know* He had chosen the wrong guy. Moses eventually came to his senses and helped God free the Israelites from Egyptian bondage. The stuttering Hebrew understood God's power but had lacked confidence that God could use him to perform the type of miracles the Lord was promising. Even though Moses did amazing wonders by God's hand, that arguing with his Creator limited Moses's ministry for the rest of his life. Our Heavenly Father wants to do more through each of our lives, if only we would ask Him to show us, and then when He does, we must respond in faith and obedience.

Like Moses, I needed more convincing that this woman God pointed out was really in His plans for me, but the meeting and my conversation with the Lord ended. So still *feeling* like God must have missed the mark on this one, I quickly exited out of the door and down a long alleyway to where the other Salvation Army guys were gathered. My mind reeled; who is this woman God pointed out? Is she really *the one*? Or just my lonely, homeless, despairing self in need of a girlfriend? What's her story? After all, she doesn't even know I exist at this point—or does she?

3

"Who Is This Woman?"

Mia

• • • • • • •

It was a bit over ten years ago that my life started becoming a serious question mark. I was a single mom with no vision or hope for the future, someone who always had to learn the hard way because of my rebellious, stubborn, and feisty disposition. Born in April during the wonderful 70s, I had amazing parents who were southern, blue-collar folks. I'm the middle child with two brothers, and I felt like I was part of a magnificent family. Though identifying as Christian, I was always more spiritual than religious, which helped me justify *only* hanging out with drinkers, pot smokers, or harder-drug users. Unlike me, most of my open-minded and non-judgmental "friends" did not overindulge and confessed to "love" me for who I was, meaning they never warned me or condemned my reckless, experimental, dangerous behavior.

On May 10th, 2010, as a stay-at-home mom my toxic lifestyle finally pushed me to the limit. I acknowledged having lost all sense of reality, checked into rehab, and vowed never to drink alcohol again—I was serious! I had caused enough emotional pain for my children and me. My two boys were young. They needed a safe mom. . .and a present one. I was neither. Though not out nights partying, unlike controlled drinkers my home-alone indulging had long since gone beyond one glass of wine.

Drinking had been common in my high school, but from my first teenage drink, I drank alcoholically. My crowd brought booze to every sort of occasion, so until age thirty-nine I overindulged more times than not. I hadn't planned to lose control and ruin my kids' lives, but there I was—and May 10th would not be my last attempt to stop drinking. I kept trying to limit myself to one drink, but eventually could no longer live with the person I had become, finally reaching a place of spiritual desolation where I was completely separated from the giver of life, God. I was a shallow shell of a human, of little help to myself or anyone.

Two years later my life forever changed on May 14th, 2012. Looking in the mirror I knew in the pit of my dark soul that God had not created me to be this person. That probably sounds familiar because Robby's awakening was almost identical to mine. Coincidence? As you will see with the rest of this book, there is no such thing as coincidence!

Like Robby would eleven months later, I too cried out to Him in full surrender, hoping to be permanently changed, and though the transformation did not happen instantly—with a flash of light or a burning bush appearing in my bathroom—I was changed on the inside. The previous thirst for alcohol became a craving for my Heavenly Father, Jesus, and the Living Water (the Holy Spirit who lives inside every believer).

With my rededication to Jesus in the spring of 2012, I plunged into the Waters, committed to a close relationship with my Creator and Savior. During the first year I experienced a lot of supernatural "God-incidents" (again, after so many you must conclude they cannot be just coincidences). A *huge* one was how I no longer woke up craving alcohol; instead, my soul continued healing, which led to feeling more and more alive! Near the beginning of my rededicated walk with Jesus, He revealed this important truth in Matthew 7:13–14:

> *"Enter through the narrow gate. For wide is the gate and broad is the road that leads to destruction, and many enter through it. But small is the gate and narrow the road that leads to life, and only a few find it."*

Along those lines, the Holy Spirit impressed upon me that we are meant to keep a short distance—the narrow road—between our head and heart. Only having knowledge of God's Word isn't enough if that understanding is not connected to your heart, the part of you that decides whether to walk out biblical wisdom, or not. I was *so* ready to do it God's way. Picking up my cross and following Jesus!

Continuing in close relationship with the Lord, I began thriving while my boys slowly got back to feeling safer and trusting me again. God was showing me areas of my life where I had been deceived, and how He protected me through my horrible behavior. From this new place of growing joy and freedom, I promised God I would remain single, committing my life to more deeply knowing Him. Up to that point I had never been happier. Other than the boys' activities or attending church and meetings, my evenings were mostly spent at home, sitting on the pool deck worshiping God under the stars, bonding with my Savior, becoming the daughter He created me to be and the godly mother my children deserved.

One day while frantically juggling dishes, laundry, and a few other chores, I was pausing to remember what came next when I suddenly felt prompted to address God instead:

"Lord, I am all over the place today. What do you want me to do? Who am I? Who did you create me to be? I know you have something specific you want me to do today, so what is it?"

His answer changed my life forever! God had recently seemed to show His love for me through sightings of hearts, whether with a cloud, stone, leaf, or even something like an oil stain. Knowing that, the Holy Spirit must have subconsciously led me to my closet. There I reached up to my purses and grabbed a white one with pink hearts. The hearts felt like a sign, but the much more significant part was that I had never seen that bag before. A bit stunned, I opened it to figure out where it might have come from, and the mystery continued when I found a book inside. It was *When a Woman Discovers Her Dream,* by Cindi McMenamin. Shocked, amazed, and curious, I knelt by the bed and began to read the paperback that appeared to have never been opened. Even today, I can only assume it was divinely placed there for me to find at that time.

For much of my life I had felt distracted, so this helpful tool was something needed, and that divinely delivered gift was just the start of God's significant communication to come. There by the bed as I began reading, the Spirit of God fell on me. I started weeping, and my whole life changed. Without a doubt, I knew in that moment that Jesus was calling me to serve Him in a life of Christian ministry.

The book details how the enemy targets us, wanting desperately to snuff out the purpose God placed inside us before birth. The deceiver wants to snatch our dreams, subtly derailing and twisting us around until we are moving in the opposite direction from the Lord's purpose. I needed to become persistently dedicated to discovering and fulfilling my destiny, a task that only takes picking up God's Road map: a steady study of Scripture will always supply the right road toward your unique God-ordained purpose. On this day, many of my deepest, most heartfelt concerns and questions were suddenly answered and erased. I was on my way to learning, understanding, and reaching my dreams.

I grew up in South Georgia, where we lived in a small town and attended a Southern Baptist church, where I gave my heart to Jesus at six years old. Some may say six is too young to know the truth, and considering my rebellious, alcoholic-soaked life that followed, I might tend to agree, but that's not the character of the God we serve. When you believe Jesus is who He says, and you sincerely ask Him to come into your heart, Christ will do so and then wait for you to seek Him with your whole heart. Now that I have a fuller love in my heart for Jesus, I know He has resided there from childhood.

For many years my family was involved with our little tight-knit church, a place of pleasant memories where I would worship with the congregation and spend time in the church prayer closet, a room way up in a steeple with beautiful stained-glass windows—I loved and still love that secret place. I am only still alive today because God remained by my side through the worst depths of my depravity, waiting for me to turn back toward Him. Only His will and endless love allow you and me to continue living at this moment; as long as we have breath, the Lord is not finished with us.

God waits to create a new life in His children, and sometimes that means bringing us back full circle. As a child I had a fire inside that burned with passion for Him, often spending hours in my room, lining up my baby dolls, and then blasting them with some of the finest gospel preaching in Georgia; that is, judging by their enthusiastic, wide-eyed expressions. Unlike Christians, apparently figurines can lose their salvation: those little dolls got saved over and over and over.

One day at Sunday school, the teacher walked out of the room while we were all lined up against the wall eating our snacks (I can still taste those small butter cookies with a hole in the middle, the ones I loved to dip in red Kool-Aid). As we all ate with the teacher absent, I took that opportunity to continue the other children's education—God wanted their little hearts!

Today, my brothers and I are testaments to my parents laying the foundation of Christianity, as Scripture prescribes in Proverbs 22:6:

> "Train up a child in the way he should go; even when he is old
> he will not depart from it."

Family only comes second to God, and since I reengaged, my entire family faithfully serves Jesus. I am thankful for their obedience and feel blessed to have grown up when strong morals and values were still widespread, virtues I have been able to pass to my boys.

By twenty years old I had moved out of small-town Georgia and into the metropolitan area of Tampa, St. Pete, and Clearwater, Florida. Because I was rebellious, high school had not been important to me, so of course

I was not interested in attending college; instead, I married young and made the best two decisions of my life. By age twenty-six I had given birth to a couple of baby boys. And they were miracles. Before either was born, doctors had informed my husband he faced zero ability to help conceive a biological child. But even having heard that, deep inside I *knew* we would be blessed with kids. As a married stay-at-home mom to two amazing little boys, life could not have been better. My dream of being a wife and mother had come true. In fact, I had never desired to be anything else. Despite not having the large number of children I wanted, we were a couple with two kids, a dog, a beautiful home, a swimming pool, and an actual white picket fence—we were living the American dream.

But as years passed and the God-sized hole in my soul remained empty, I tried filling it with life's pleasures and expectations. Being greatly deceived about my true godly purpose, it wasn't long until our marriage ended. Even with that enormous, traumatic change, I was abundantly blessed to continue staying at home with my boys. However, a lot of emotional issues began for me as they got older and more independent; I developed fears and insecurities about "only" being a mother with no valuable career or important title. What would be my purpose after they move out and I'm no longer a stay-at-home mom—my heart's core desire for my whole life! As the anxiety creeped in more and more, even living the mother life was starting to feel like being stuck in mundane tasks. I had no future vision, so all I knew to do was celebrate life through worldly pleasures and passions.

Raising godly kids is monumentally important for the children, grandchildren, society, and the Lord's kingdom, but I began to see it less as a gift and more like a failed life, buying into the lie that I was *just* a stay-at-home mom. We were comfortable and their father was an excellent provider, but I knew the mother season would end and I would be too old to start a career. What could it even be? I had no vision. No desires. No passions. By this time the questions were haunting me: Who starts a career or goes back to school in their 40s? Should I have been saving instead of spending so much? Isn't my house too big for one person? Can I even do life on my own? These thoughts were racing through my mind, and it became daily, eventually causing debilitating fear from feelings of worthlessness, self-pity, regret, anxiety, and every other demonic attack.

This was when my social drinking turned to having alcohol every day, embracing my crutch that eventually led to isolation from everyone I love—it was insanity! People seek pleasure and avoid pain, especially when faced with fear and insecurity. God gave us feelings because we are made in His image and He is Love, but the enemy uses *temporary* feeling (just something you feel for a bit) to have us believe lies. Those issues can quickly pass, but the deceiver is after the souls of non-believers and the witnessing efforts of Christians, so he constantly fans the anxiety flames to hijack our minds, allowing him to control our behavior.

For a brief time while struggling to find my purpose, I took an interest in the spiritual New Age movement. I naively used New Age (westernized Hinduism) methods involving ungodly spirit guides and other pagan practices like crystals, tarot cards, yoga, reiki, meditation, and many related forms of dark spiritualism. This was a very dark time in my life. *Please* see the addendum at the end of this book to better understand the extreme dangers of New Age. The enemy's elaborate, powerful deception twisted my perception of reality into an all-consuming identity *crisis*.

And he wanted more than just me; he used me to get to my children, and if he had been able to keep me separated from God, I shudder to think where my beautiful family might be—or not be—today. If the boys were even able to survive the alcohol-impaired driving, my constant intoxication would have continued the shallow, fearful, regretful, inconsistent behavior, producing hurt and angry teens who would have become toxically resentful young men. But praise God that my recklessness was met with the Lord's intervening grace that kept us safe until my sanity returned. Also, had I not reversed my worldly focus, the other tragedy would have been my boys missing a demonstration of Christ's redemptive work on the cross and the joy of a life lived with Jesus.

4

"Nice Bracelet"

More than a year had passed since rededicating my life to Jesus—my Lord, Savior, and best friend. I was full of exes: exhilarated, excited, exuberant, and extremely joyful. I had been profoundly transformed forever.

The boys were spending every weekend with their father, and Sunday night to Friday afternoon with me. I loved being a stay-at-home mom and would not have traded even a minute spent with my boys for anything in the world. That said, some of you know how five and a half days with teenagers can feel like a lot longer. I was blessed to be a full-time mom *and* have solitude on the weekends. Of course, I was no longer going out drinking, socializing, and dating; I wanted uninterrupted time with Jesus. He and I were having nice dinners, worship parties, Bible studies, "tear-fests," swings in the hammock (next to the pool under the stars), and some late-night swims. I had never done well alone, but now I was loving it. While I was not worried about finding *the one*, God was teaching me how to just let Him love on me.

But I was unprepared for what was coming in late July of 2013, the personal earthquake that led me to a whole new level of Christian experience (and eventually this book). My formerly wrecked, alcoholic existence had become content, full, and peaceful. My whole life felt in balance, or so I thought. God had something else in store. Though I felt my life could not get better, God had greater blessings planned, as He promises to those who will walk closely with Him:

> *"And we know that in all things God works for the good of those who love him, who have been called according to his purpose."* (Romans 8:28)

"If God is for us, who can be against us? He who did not spare his own Son, but gave him up for us all—how will he not also, along with him, graciously give us all things?"
(Romans 8:31–32)

" 'For I know the plans I have for you,' declares the Lord, 'plans to prosper you. . .' "
(Jeremiah 29:11)

By prospering us, He's not promising to make us all rich; shallow materialism does not provide happiness. Glorifying God in a close relationship with Him brings us the fruits of the Spirit, including joy that lasts.

I was quickly awakening to God and His plans for my life. At this point I knew I was called to ministry, so I registered for Bible college. Though I didn't know specifically where my studies would lead, I was hungry for God, His Word, and whatever He had for me. There were long dormant parts of me coming alive daily, developments that drove me more and more toward serving the Lord with all my heart and soul. Though I had no details of what that service would entail, I knew I would never make another important decision without first prayerfully seeking God's face, constantly asking His will. This godly attitude kept me open to receive God's help with my mind, heart, soul, and spirit. Eventually I would learn that His plans for me were somehow related to Genesis 2:18:

"It is not good that man should be alone; I will make a helper suitable for him."

The full context tells us that *suitable* refers to whether the helper is *right* and *appropriate* for a particular person, as well as their purpose and situation.

With a life-changing day in late July rapidly approaching, as I confessed earlier, remaining alone had become important to me. And the Lord knew it. I had been relishing my uninterrupted time with God. Had He asked if I wanted to keep it that way—which He didn't—I would have suggested He not mess up my wonderful life by matchmaking. Of course, He knew better. What do I know? Relatively nothing.

Friday, July 26th, was the typical tropical sauna that is summer in Tampa, Florida. I had made myself a promise to be in my life's best spiritual and physical shape by forty, the age I had turned that past April. I had achieved many personal goals, including a year of sobriety and experiencing the presence of God like never before.

An example of those divinely orchestrated experiences led me to an encounter with a young woman named Tiffany. One day after a service at Grace Family Church (just before my fortieth birthday in early spring), they were holding their monthly baptisms, a joyous event the whole congregation is invited to. I had never stayed for it, but this day the Holy Spirit prompted me to go watch. As I stood taking in the beautiful professions of faith, a young woman walked down the steps and into the water. The pastor prayed and then baptized her. As she came out of the water, I too felt like someone had just poured warm water over my head, and it was now running down, all the way to the soles of my feet. Weeping from an overwhelming presence of the Spirit, I knew God wanted me to meet her.

The church supplies clean clothes for those unprepared for baptism (because they made a lastminute decision), so I waited until she came out of the dressing room and introduced myself. She smiled, giggled a bit, said hello, and let me know her name was Tiffany. As we talked, I learned she too had been struggling for freedom from alcohol addiction.

Tiffany and I developed a unique friendship over the next few months. Together we even set up a Bible study based on *The Purpose Driven Life*, by Rick Warren. Every time I encountered an individual the Lord wanted me to invite, I'd tell them to pray about it and let me know. It was always the same response: I don't need to pray about it, I have the book and have been wanting to do this Bible study. The experience was Holy Spirit led, and I'm still amazed how the Lord made that happen.

Although Tiffany had small victories in her recovery, we lost her halfway through the course. Still, soon after, she and I got involved with other Bible studies. As she struggled, I wanted desperately to help, so I invited her to stay with me a few days; this way we could attend AA meetings and read Scripture together. On a side note, Tiffany has one of the most angelic voices I have ever heard, God's anointing that breaks the enemy's chains, which has always made her a prime target to be led astray and silenced by the devil.

Because Tiffany was staying with me and she desperately needed AA meetings, I vowed to take her to a few; otherwise, I would not have attended that meeting on July 26th: I had previously planned to meet my neighbor Valerie—my best friend on earth—and then attend a prayer vigil with her at Grace Family Church. But God changed my plans to taking Tiffany to the AA meeting and then going with Valerie to the prayer vigil.

Like most Friday nights, the AA room was full. We walked in late, quietly took our seats, and because the message had no personal application with my family, I vaguely remember it being about people who had lost parents or other loved ones.

Once the speaker was finished, we meandered out the door and cheerfully walked through the parking lot to where a group of Salvation Army guys were gathered talking. Because we were already friends with many of them, we approached to join in the conversation—but then I noticed someone new—and he was wearing my exact same *Better Together* bracelet! Being a bit bold, I reached toward his wrist from behind and popped it, while playfully exclaiming:

"Nice bracelet!"

He turned with somewhat of a strange smirk. It felt sort of flirty, like he had been expecting me. Kind of perplexed at the reaction, I continued with a question:

"Do you go to Grace Family Church?"

With a slight stutter he answered:

"Yes. . .I do."

I told him we were about to head there for a prayer vigil, and then he took me off guard again with his quick response:

"I wish I could go with you guys."

Not willing to entertain a homeless rehab stranger possibly asking for a ride, I deflected:

"I have never seen you here before."

His reply was surprisingly stern:

"And you probably never will again: I am working my recovery with my Lord and Savior Jesus Christ."

Wonderful, I thought, and then gleefully added:

"Me too!"

After I said that, his head seemed to drop in disbelief, which puzzled me. Then a bit of that smirk reappeared, and he mentioned that I reminded him of someone—but did not care to elaborate. So, we said goodbye and he hopped on the Salvation Army bus. Tiffany and I left to pick up Valerie for the prayer vigil.

I can still remember our excitement that night, feeling like we were going to meet Jesus. We prayed for three straight hours and then floated out of the sanctuary—a most amazing feeling. Though I was not willing to give him a ride, for some reason I felt led to pray for the AA guy I had met earlier. But I would often pray for strangers, and I hadn't thought much more about him, maybe because of the jeans, black cowboy boots, and black vest—not my type of attire. Besides, despite what might have been his flirty interest, I was off the market. Whether he cared or not, for the first time in my life I was *not* looking or hoping for Mr. Right, Mr. Gonna-Fix-Me, Mr. Complete-Me, Mr. Make-Me-Happy, or anyone else. Jesus had done all that, so I certainly wasn't looking for a man to mess that up, especially a possibly recovering addict living at the Salvation Army.

The following day was also everything I anticipated and much, much more. Valerie and I were excited to attend a luncheon with the Bible-study people we had met the week prior, a time to know them better, learn more, and find out what God was doing with all of us. After sitting, listening, and understanding that the ministry was something special, Valerie and I went out for gelato—also heavenly. There we ran into some of the Bible study people, including the pastor and his wife. Following some small talk, his wife suddenly looked at me and declared:

"You need to get your notebook ready. The Lord will be speaking to you."

Anticipation shot through my spirit, confirming that her two sentences were a word from the Lord. I could not have imagined so much excitement coming into my life, but I would come to learn that these sorts of mind-blowing experiences are normal when walking closely with Christ—just read Bible history.

5

"Meeting on Holy Grounds and Holy Ground"

What a wonderful day so far, and God had much more planned for me: at the Grace Family Church evening service, Valerie and I were standing in the coffee line and guess who walked into the lobby. It was the Salvation Army guy. He and Kevin, a man I had met at prior AA meetings, came straight over to the church coffee shop. They were headed to the back of the line when Kevin saw me and spoke up, calling me Missy and mentioning that I reminded him of a friend back home. Pointing at the other guy, I replied:

"Oh, yeah? He says I remind him of someone too."

I struggled for a moment to recall his name and then added:

"Robby, right?"

That recollection had to be help from the Holy Spirit because I have always been bad with names, though I'm trying to get better. He replied:

"Good memory, Mia. You remembered my name."

I mentioned me reminding Robby of someone because curiosity gripped me that night we met, when he seemed secretive about it. Kevin's comment gave me the chance to pursue the subject:

"So, Robby, who do I remind you of?"

He dropped his head like the other night, and answered with what almost looked like despair:

"The one that got away. . ."

That explained the other night. Valerie and I grabbed our coffee and headed into the sanctuary and being early we were able to sit in the second row. Pretty soon I heard a now-familiar voice directly behind:

"Do you have to sit right in front of me?"

I turned around to see Robby—with that same smirk! I said, "No, I don't," and we moved to another area; it was clear by the way he said it that I was a distraction, something I certainly did not want to be for anyone listening to a message about God. Once the service concluded, the usual huge crowd shuffled out into the lobby and through the various doors on each side. Normally there are volunteers holding the doors open, but not that night, for some reason. So, I held the door for a couple who came behind me and ended up getting stuck there. Even with the packed lobby spilling out, I noticed Robby walking toward me—and then he veered toward the other set of doors. I jokingly called to him:

"Are you too good to come through my door?"

Seemingly caught off guard, he appeared shocked at my question and a bit speechless. Then he shyly responded:

"No, not at all. I didn't see you."

Yeah, right. He walked over to his group of friends, most of whom I knew from the AA program, so as soon as the flow of people subsided, I joined them; we were all acquaintances, and it would have been unusual if I hadn't. After some small talk, Robby asked if I would like to meet him later for coffee or come do karaoke with his group. I did not feel the least bit interested in karaoke, but there was still something tempting about it that I could not explain. I had to take Valerie home and walks the dogs, so I told him I would pray about it, and he may or may not see me.

6

"Notebook in Hand"

It was another hot, sticky, muggy evening in July, a season that often means more than one bath, shower, or dip in the pool per day. I started the bathwater, turned on my radio nearby, and then questioned the Lord out loud:

"I don't know why I am even considering going to meet Robby, but do you want me to?"

My spirit heard a clear answer:

"No, you have been busy all week and I need time alone with you."

That was the week Tiffany had been staying with me to help her get on the sobriety path, so these were my first few minutes alone without her or the boys. I felt the presence of God stirring, so I turned off the bathwater and radio, walked over to put away my jewelry, and was pushing the drawer shut when I was immediately hit by a download from heaven. With the Holy Spirit in my life, there had been many supernatural experiences, but this was something new. I recalled earlier when the pastor's wife prophesied that I must get my notebook ready because the Lord was going to start speaking to me. So, I grabbed a notebook and my laptop, sat at the kitchen table, and proceeded to write everything I was hearing in my spirit. It's hard to explain if you have not been through this, but I knew what I was supposed to write. While doing so, I felt led to play *Amazing Grace*, so I googled it and played the first one my eyes gravitated to, a beautiful version with bagpipes.

Then the strangest thing happened: not long after getting back to writing, I suddenly found myself in the refrigerator with my hand in a bowl of blueberries. I thought:

"I'm not even hungry. This is clearly the enemy's way of distracting me from what God is trying to show me."

Food is a simple way for the deceiver to distract us. Excited about this movement of God, I knew Valerie too had been diligently seeking Him for answers and direction in her own life, so I thought He must also be speaking clearly to my best friend around this time. She and I were baptized and prayed together, shared Scripture, laughed, cried, and were both desperate to hear His voice above all the noise in this world. So, I ran next door to tell her that God was speaking to me, and she needed to get ready because he would surely be speaking to her soon.

Within minutes of me leaving her house, Valerie randomly decided to come over and play with my dogs—that was the first and only time I ever asked her to leave. After distracting blueberries and taking a writing break to prepare her for a download from God, I had gotten back to scribbling down all I was hearing from the Lord. It was all good though; we laughed as I kicked her all the way to the door and out of my house, saying:

"Listen, I love you, but you've got to go!"

That night I kept writing what the Holy Spirit was revealing, and I still revisit it today as His master plan for me continues unfolding. So far, I don't fully understand half of it, but God and His Word have helped me somewhat piece the mystery together. Many years later my life does not look exactly like what He wrote through me, but much is close and more comes to fruition as I continue seeking God's will—and the same is available to every Christian.

That week I felt the Lord leading me to pray for Robby every day. Again, this was not unusual. God was often placing people in my path and putting them on my heart to pray for. Some I may never speak with, and others became a significant part of my life. I asked the Heavenly Father to reveal Himself to Robby, touch him, and bless him. Those prayers for this man I barely knew were quite specific and intentional. During some of those prayers, I told God that I would continue to do so for Robby, even though the Lord had not told me why he needed it.

I did not know what to do with all the new information from the writing download, but I was happy to be patient and enjoy joyful days with my home life back on track after giving up booze for Jesus—that's what happens, praise God! On Sundays at dinner time, the boys would come home from their dad's house, which allowed me to continue our undistracted, face-to-face talks at mealtimes, an important tradition my entire life. By this time, we were settled into our summer routine where the boys ate a lot, stayed up late, and slept until noon. That worked well with my mornings being devoted to Christ, errands, and the gym: I could still make it home to cook them "breakfast." Cooking is my favorite hobby and feeding the boys has brought me much joy! Besides my relationship with God, being a mom has by far provided my greatest accomplishments and happiness.

When I think about the wonderful transformation God has given me—even after my life of horrible, rebellious behavior—it still blows my mind to think how the deceiver was keeping me and my boys away from so much heaven on earth. There were times during addiction where I no longer cooked, exercised, or even spent time with family or friends. The enemy had completely deceived me into isolation, steeling away my God-given gifts of serving and cooking, not to mention losing all desire to live, love, and laugh. I was never suicidal, but I did die inside. I bought into falsehoods constantly whispered in my ear by the thief who comes only to steal, kill, and destroy. The enemy had me feeling like a failure, not only from alcoholism, but also because he convinced me that mom-work was of no value. Looking back, that was such a ridiculous lie. And it was I who allowed that treatment from the enemy, just because I had no significant interest in my Creator, Savior, and the Source of all joy. Now I am renewed daily by the truth of God's Word, as explained with this commentary on Isaiah 55:10–11:

> " 'As the rain cometh down, and the snow from heaven, . . .
> So shall my word be that goeth forth out of my mouth: it shall
> not return unto me void.' The word void means 'empty.' The
> remainder of verse 11 explains what it means to 'not return
> void,' saying that God's Word 'will accomplish what I desire
> and achieve the purpose for which I sent it.' "[1]

You and I are who God says we are—period—we are no longer bound to the ways of this world, thank God!

Anyone with kids understands how much I have *always* loved and wanted to protect my children, which reveals the insidiousness of addiction. Even with that unbreakable momma-bear devotion, I put those little guys through a couple years of my corrupting nonsense. Now into recovery for about half that time, and even though my example was monumentally better, our new Jesus life took them time getting used to. Again, our family professed Christ as Savior, attended church, and even prayed at home, but I demonstrated a parent who had fallen away from God and did not know what Jesus did for humanity. That large chunk of their childhood left the boys leery that any day, hypocrisy-mom might rear her inconsistent head again.

Today we thank God for His grace and love that have flooded my children's hearts, making our home a true example of what it's like to live life in Christ. This may sound like a social media page where the dirt is

---

1 https://www.gotquestions.org/not-return-void.html

never disclosed, and the only information posted testifies to a perfect family. Yes, we will all have problems with sin until Jesus returns, but I have seen my young men grow to exemplify grace, love, and forgiveness. Our home is not perfect. Not by any means. But it's God's house. Permeated with His presence.

During my entire recovery up to this point, I had been enjoying many types of God gatherings that always provided a biblical gold nugget or two, and the Lord met me every Friday night at the AA meetings. Another AA meeting approached as I finished a week of seeking God's revelations about my Holy Spirit writing, while also continuing to pray daily for Robby, someone I may not see again. But it sure seemed like God was doing something around that new connection.

7

"The Call That Began It All"

Driving to the AA meeting after God had me thinking about Robby all week during prayers, I was kind of hoping to see him again. But as he had vowed when we met, he did not return. Though my flesh didn't care, something inside felt different. It wasn't like my past motivations that were dominated by fleshly desires; I was 100% surrendered to the Holy Spirit—the opposite influence. Being alone, I was happy, content, and really did not think about getting into a relationship, especially with some guy in rehab.

But again, there was some sort of inner feeling involved, maybe involving my spirit. Months prior, the Holy Spirit said something confusing, telling me to behave as a mother—*and wife*. Having been a single mom for quite some time, I took that to mean no dating because the Lord wanted me to focus on the boys and my growing relationship with Him. Or maybe it was about a future reconciliation in my marriage.

As I was exiting the AA meeting, Brian from the Salvation Army group walked up, held out a piece of paper, and explained:

"Robby would like you to call him, but he understands if you don't."

I quickly reached for the note and told him:

"Give it to me. It's God!"

I knew it in my heart, and even Brian thought so. I had just met him at the noon meeting that Wednesday. Some of us would often get lunch together after those meetings, so since Brian was new, I invited him to come along. At first, he declined, but then showed up. Later he confessed that his plan had been to get drunk that afternoon and how he probably would have if I had not asked him to eat with us. I am happy to report that

Brian is still sober and doing amazingly well.

Normally I would not have called the same night, but having learned that these encounters were God things, I knew the Lord wanted me to call Robby right away. As usual, those of us exiting the meeting talked outside for quite a while, but as soon as we said our goodbyes, I hopped in the car, prayed, and then dialed Robby's number.

It felt like we had known each other all of our lives. We talked on the phone for what seemed like hours, with no dull moments and so much laughter. We confirmed plans to spend the next day together, first hanging out at my community clubhouse pool, for which I would pick him up—the man had no wheels!!—and then we would go to *our* church. Though he was without a car, a job, or even a home, the material world no longer motivated me. Besides, I knew God was in this budding friendship. The fact that Robby was living in a hopeless place (or was he?) did not scare me in the least. I knew we had two crucial passions in common: Jesus and sobriety.

That said, I was concerned about possibly harming his recovery: anyone who knows anything about addiction understands that dating during rehab is a huge no-no. Having attended so many AA meetings, I was certainly aware. However, we were not the typical addicts. God was in control of our situations. Like Robby, I too was working my recovery through our Lord and Savior Jesus Christ, and in that close walk with God, I knew to seek His will and way on every decision. He would *not* lead me astray.

But anything the Lord puts together, the enemy schemes to twist and pervert, so I also understood any collaboration to advance God's kingdom would be an important time to discern schemes of the deceiver. And I would not leave my God-path for anything. I had been there. It is horrible. I chose Jesus.

Even with that godly focus, this period would begin a year of the most serious spiritual fight I have ever gone through. God had miraculously transformed my life from depression brought on by my pathetic behavior to a new joyous life walking with the Lord, but I still worried about struggles I had when I was worldly and willingly living separate from the will of God. My new challenge involved a fear of making a wrong decision, potentially separating myself from the Lord's desires for my life. I had developed a true aversion to doing wrong in His eyes.

8

"Take 'em to Church"

The next morning, I awoke with more excitement about the day ahead than I wanted to have. I was cautiously curious about what God was up to, and I knew He wanted me to show Robby the previous week's note-writing vision. Also, on our call he expressed disappointment that I had not shown up at karaoke, but it hadn't been the right time to explain, so I would get that chance today.

All that enthusiasm went out the window at 8:30am when Robby called. After he talked with me, his rehab accountability group gave him a hard time—and rightly so—about making plans to be with me all day. Before our conversation, Robby had committed to attend church with some newer men at the Salvation Army who were looking up to him for their accountability. Because he was somewhat of a mentor and their example for how to do rehab, bailing on them for a date would be terrible. Again, dating during the first year of recovery through AA and NA (Narcotics Anonymous) programs is strongly discouraged. Finances and romances can quickly take a person out.

Well aware of that, my service-minded motivation through recovery had been to help anyone in need who came along—that's what we are supposed to do. And I had helped many by that time, so rather than think about a possible intimate relationship, my focus with Robby was on a new friendship with someone who was seriously seeking the same sober and spiritual path. Robby's godly approach was refreshing since few seek Jesus in recovery (unfortunately), and I could hear how he really wanted to become a man of honor again. Alcoholism, drug addiction, and other sins rob us of virtue. Rather than being out to "score a date," Robby wanted to recover his integrity. Either way though, "scoring" was unlikely in his current financial situation. God allowed us to connect because He knew we were both earnestly trying to live like Christ. But again, it is always important to keep an eye on our motivations possibly being influenced by the sneaky enemy.

After hanging up the phone, I began seeking the face of God with my spirit overflowing. Suddenly the Holy Spirit offered a solution:

"Take them all to church."

Brilliant idea, God! I called Robby and offered to haul the whole group of Salvation Army guys to church; that is, if he still wanted to spend the day together at my community pool. Besides, I certainly would not have brought him to my house, so he would need to be dropped off at his homeless home to shower and change before church. He agreed and I immediately headed out the door to get him. During that whole drive I wondered what in the world I was thinking, picking up this guy I barely knew. Still, my decades of being off God's path had me seriously scared of countering His will, and He surely had some reason for this man and me to connect.

Since we had discovered that we both liked energy drinks, I grabbed a couple on the way and soon pulled into the parking lot of Robby's building. There he stood out front—with that same smirk on his face! I was becoming quite curious about this frequent expression but would not find out why he had it until much later. The answer was worth waiting for. . .a life-altering doozy!. . .a God thing!

He jumped in the car, and we headed to my clubhouse pool. The previous night's conversation continued since we had much to talk about with all the Lord had done in our lives, including how we were both grateful to even be alive after our decades of horrible behavior. Time often seems to stand still when discussing aspects of a God-centered life. With no dull moments that day, our fellowship flowed perfectly—led by the Holy Spirit.

Robby
• • • • • • • •

As Mia mentioned, we were continuing our conversation from the night before, and I was excited to learn what she needed to share with me— though I added that it *must* be delivered in person. It wasn't long before she decided to tell me, but with the caveat that she hoped it would not freak me out. I let her know I could say the same thing about what I was holding back. She summed it up for both of us by disclosing how God revealed that she and I would be doing something together for Christ. Though this was expected, her saying so set my heart pounding. I urgently wanted to confirm her statement by relaying how God told me *you're the one!*—but this being our first date, the Holy Spirit would have none of that; I was told to remain silent.

Mia went on to share her God-given download that happened the night she was a no-show for karaoke. Praise God that Christ was and still is more important to Mia than I am. I got "God bumps" hearing Mia explain how the Lord revealed aspects of my future role in her life, like how we would do recovery ministry together. This resonated that God would enlist my future partner to help me aid those suffering addiction, and she too understood that the ultimate recovery plan is provided by Christ's gospel.

When she had finished, the Holy Spirit prompted me to share the most intimate dream of my life, one I had four years earlier and never mentioned to anyone. Feeling comfortable, vulnerable, and transparent with Mia, I recounted the vision that startled me awake at 3am (long before becoming a Christian):

> "I saw Jesus coming in the clouds, ascending to earth with His arms stretched wide. No longer able to stand, I fell to my knees but continued looking up as I realized the entire planet could also see Him. That was when I suddenly awoke and sat straight up in my bed—every hair on my body was standing on end."

Here's what is truly amazing: just a few weeks later, Mia and I were in the middle of an intimate, Holy Spirit-filled conversation when she felt led to read from the book of Revelation. Mainly because of my brief walk of faith up to that point, Mia knew my Bible exposure so far was mostly the four Gospels and a few epistles. She began reading from the first chapter of Revelation, and I burst into tears when she got to verse 7:

> "Behold, He is coming with the clouds, and every eye will see Him—even those who pierced Him. And all the tribes of the earth will mourn because of Him. So shall it be! Amen."

Wow! Even before I made the decision to follow God (with all my heart and soul), in a dream He revealed Himself to me. Then years later, not surprisingly He used Mia to give me the corresponding biblical revelation from His book of Revelation.

I went on to tell Mia how—as a worldly businessman—I had been the farthest thing from a believer, and shortly after the dream, I got injured, which led to severe drug addiction that nearly took my life. Now having accepting Christ, I believe that dark period was about the enemy trying to silence me before I could glorify God by telling anyone the vivid dream. Mia would later confess to becoming engrossed in my story, and that day we both realized our mutual sharing of intimate details had not freaked either of us out. In fact, we now understand how the Holy Spirit controlled that day's pool conversation; He was using it to give us an enticing glimpse into our future together.

Considering the topic had already come up in the church coffee line, further discussion of my ex-girlfriend Michelle was inevitable. Mia remembered how Michelle reminded me of her, which made Mia want to learn the intimate details. After I told her about Michelle, Mia cautioned that my characterization of her as "the one" might mean I still have a soul tie to Michelle, so maybe I should consider asking God for deliverance. I had no clue what she meant by a soul tie or deliverance, and I so wanted to tell Mia that Michelle was no longer even a possibility because God picked Mia out for this broken, broke, homeless addict. But it was still too soon. Next, I asked Mia if she was seeing anyone, to which she responded with a resounding:

"No way!"

Her answer gave me hope, but she knew her reaction was a bit strong, so she explained that her all-encompassing relationship with Christ had become most important—as it had for me. Mia was also honest about her ex-husband being a large part of her and her boys' lives. In fact, she had come to understand the marriage-destroying deception she had participated in. And their relationship was friendly, so Mia was willing to reconcile for the sake of the boys, even though her and her ex-husband's paths were no longer the same. She knew God could do anything. Obviously, that caused my heart to sink, but I knew her efforts to preserve their godly union were biblically sound. Unfortunately, though, if the Lord was going to put them back together, then she would not be the one for me—as God promised. So, I silently challenged my Heavenly Father:

"Lord, why would You bring her into my life if she may reconcile with her ex-husband?"

Somewhat dispelling *my* concerns (not God's), Mia added that her ex-husband was in a committed relationship so she could not see how getting back together might even be possible. Nonetheless, a potential rival was tough to hear about, but the situation helped us become close friends before any sort of intimacy. We each put Jesus at the center of our lives, and since God brought us together to do His will—not ours—we would both stay the course for whatever He desired. When our pool time ended, Mia dropped me off at the Salvation Army, and then came back a couple hours later to take a few of us beneficiaries to church. Driving there with Mia, I felt relaxed knowing God was at the center of our relationship and we were allowing the Holy Spirit to guide.

At church we sat next to each other, which allowed me to lean her way a bit, close my eyes, and breathe. . . Mia smelled amazing! My job at the Salvation Army was putting price tags on clothing destined for thrift stores. Items were often donated without being washed by the last person to wear them, something probably done by people reading this—you know who you are—*lol!* This meant work included a variety of lotion and perfume smells. My favorite was coconut, so wouldn't it be just like God to give me the desires of my heart. As I sat appreciating Mia's choice of fragrance, she caught me inhaling and asked what I was doing. A bit embarrassed, I confessed she smelled nice, but I didn't elaborate. Mia rolled her wrists over to reveal a couple tattoos. The left said *Breathe*. Her right was *Faith*. Without her even knowing, God was speaking; I was listening. How's that for God's awesome sense of humor. Apparently, I was so concentrated on listening to Mia at the pool that I missed the tattoos.

Though Pastor Craig Altman is a magnificent man of God with a mighty gift for biblical teaching, I was distracted and don't remember much of the sermon that day, except for another embarrassment from a side comment I made to Mia. Pastor Craig mentioned the scriptural phrase *fear of the Lord and* being an immature Christian I mentioned to her that I did *not* fear God. Mia sat back and cocked her head toward me with a look of disbelief. I went on digging a deeper hole by declaring that the Lord I serve is a loving God, so I have no need to fear Him. Having walked with God since she was a small child, Mia recognized that I did not understand how a *reverent* fear of the Lord is the beginning of wisdom. But instead of subjecting me to some deserved ridicule, she took the opportunity to demonstrate God's grace and just let it go.

Mia had her hands full with this baby Christian often turning right when I should have gone left and pulling forward when I ought to have backed up. Though embarrassed when she would need to explain Scripture, I became grateful that Mia hung in and helped me go deeper into God's Word. Besides my Lord and this beautiful lady, it was at this time I also began falling in love with the unparalleled wisdom of Proverbs, a book of the Bible I've spent time in every day for the past two and a half years.

After church Mia asked about the two of us going for coffee. Since my rehab life allowed a lot of free time on the weekends, I agreed, and we dropped off the other guys at ARC. Sitting and sipping our espresso drinks, the Holy Spirit once again took control of our conversation, which meant me disclosing deeply personal information and beginning to weep. Rather than react like a worldly woman *might* and seeing this as male weakness, Mia's eyes filled with empathetic tears from having experienced similar trauma in her life. We two broken people found connection from transparency and prayed for each other to be healed.

All this detail about the growth of our relationship is meant to show how God was drawing us closer to Him, while also yoking us to each other. We headed back to the Salvation Army, hugged goodbye, and I thanked her for an incredible evening doing God's will; I told her it was the best time I'd ever had clean and sober. She smiled and replied:

"Aw, you're welcome. Me too!"

Watching her drive off, I joyfully thanked the Lord for my amazing new relationships with Him and Mia.

9

"The One"

The next day was Sunday, August 4th, 2013. I had been falling in love with Mia, but because of my lacking biblical knowledge, my growing dependence on her made me fearful. Only faith in God during those ARC months got me through so many doubts about this budding relationship. In Hebrews 11:6, our Heavenly Father's instruction book for life says we must *all* have faith:

"Without faith it is impossible to please God."

With persistent fear about how my lowly living situation was being perceived, I gained comfort from asking the Holy Spirit to continue leading my conversations with Mia. Then I called her. Faith immediately showed fruit: her excitement was evident. My fears were squashed by Mia's enthusiasm to talk with me, and the Christ-centered conversation again flowed. Each of us shared personal revelations from God's Word, and Mia's Bible knowledge was impressive, something even more enhanced recently through theology classes at Life Christian University. Her hunger and thirst for God's Word had led to intimacy with Christ, making me want what she had (daily Bible reading is key). With inferiority fears relieved, my worst remaining worry was wondering when I would slip up in an emotional moment and prematurely blurt that God told me she's the one. My great affection for Mia and desire for transparency with her made maintaining silence rough.

Mia invited me to the Bible study she loved at Tampa Christian Fellowship (TCF), a Thursday night gathering that the Holy Spirit told her we would attend together. This was my first encounter with an apostolic group that centers their study of Scripture around Jesus's twelve apostles, a Christian faith aptly explained here:

> *"Where [apostolics] differ from many evangelicals is in the Pentecostal teaching of tongues as a sign of Holy Spirit baptism and in their teaching that the ministry of apostles and prophets should never cease in the Church Age."[2]*

The Christ followers at that Bible study struck me by how loving, accepting, and biblically seasoned they were from clearly intimate relationships with Jesus. They were people from all walks of life who had a common love for the Lord, so they enjoyed getting together to look for revelations through deep dives into God's Word. Being a baby Christian, I felt like a fish out of water, but also knew this was exactly where God wanted me, in the center of His kids who were on fire for the wisdom and truth of Scripture.

Sitting there that evening singing praises to the Lord, I could sense the Holy Spirit's presence saturating the atmosphere. Then something strange happened at the end of worship: my arm brushed slightly against Mia, creating an unnatural, electrifying sensation I still can't explain. It was something much deeper than just electricity, a sort of soul and spirit connection that caused physical heat, a Holy Spirit fire drawing us nearer to each other—and more importantly, to our Lord and Savior. I could tell Mia too was perplexed by this sensation and I was excited to get her take on it later.

Not long after that interesting jolt, something else happened that I would have thought crazy only a few months prior: Pastor Sixto (Latin derivation of *sixth*) Ward walked over to impart a personal word of knowledge and *lay hands on* me. That's a Jewish custom that "dates back to Genesis. [Jewish forefather] Jacob laid hands on his children and pronounced various blessings on them."[3] This too brought a sensation hard to explain, but I felt the power of the Lord fall upon both of us as the pastor and I both began to weep. He then prophesied a circumstantially appropriate Bible passage over my life that related to the vision God gave Mia a week earlier, about how she and I would be working together for Christ, helping others break free from all kinds of addictions—not just drugs (me) and alcohol (Mia). Here is Isaiah 42:5–7, the passage Pastor Sixto chose for me that night:

> *"This is what God the LORD says—the Creator of the heavens, who stretches them out, who spreads out the earth with all that*

2 https://www.gotquestions.org/Apostolic-church.html

3 From Day 79 of the book *Wisdom in a Year: 365 Days of Questions & Answers That Will Change Your Life*, by Pastor Billy Crone of Sunrise Bible Church (Las Vegas, NV) and GetALifeMedia.com (probable publication late 2022)

springs from it, who gives breath to its people, and life to those who walk on it: 'I, the LORD, have called you in righteousness; I will take hold of your hand. I will keep you and will make you to be a covenant for the people and a light for the Gentiles, to open eyes that are blind, to free captives from prison and to release from the dungeon those who sit in darkness.' "

By this time, I knew God had me right where He wanted me, so I turned to Mia and three simple words flowed out:

"I am home!"

At the conclusion of that three-hour meeting, I joyfully thanked Mia for the faith she showed in me, bringing such a baby Christian to be with such incredibly Spirit-filled believers. That was when she asked the question I had been anticipating:

"So, when our arms touched during worship, did you feel anything unusual?"

I immediately responded:

"Oh, my—that was incredible!"

She asked for more detail so I told her that something divine seemed to have happened and my most-accurate description would be that it felt right. She agreed. But I hadn't told her my other thought, which was how that sort of electricity might be what it feels like between two people whose love is *just right*. My undisclosed feeling came from knowing God had us both in the palm of His hand, so there are no accidents. This understanding again made me want to tell Mia God chose her for me, and that He told me at the first moment I laid eyes on her. But this was not the time. She dropped me off at ARC, as I continued to resist.

As had become my custom, I started the next morning on my knees thanking God for the breath of life and lifting Mia up in prayer. My appeals on her behalf increased as my heart became more convicted of her being the one. What had supernaturally transpired between Mia and me seemed to have already elevated our intimacy to a significant level, but did Mia feel the same way? Or was she only thinking of us as casual friends who would one day do Christian work together?

Not knowing for sure, I was fearful of mentioning my love for her, let alone making the claim that God said we'd be husband and wife.

Since we beneficiaries were not allowed to have our cellphones on the job), my new routine was to make a beeline for the front desk at 4pm, pick up my phone, and call Mia. Of course, the world would see it as silly that a man over fifty would need permission to call a potential girlfriend. How pathetic must that guy be? Even Christians influenced by the world—like me at the time—would see that as a situation that no woman would want to get herself involved with. But through a supernatural faith in God, all that changes; day by day I was becoming more and more confident with who I am in Christ, making all things possible!

As always Mia seemed excited to answer my call, which told me we at least had a special relationship, even if only friends. Again, our conversation centered on Jesus and any new revelations from God's Word. Often the Holy Spirit would have me speak inspired words that answered Mia's prayers from the night before. This appeared to be another way the Lord helped Mia believe there could be more than a friendship developing between her and me, showing how God is in control—not either of us. As we hung up the phone, I was looking forward to the next night with her, just before heading out the following morning for a week in the mountains of North Carolina. Out of 150 beneficiaries, I and five others were chosen to go on the Salvation Army's annual retreat at Lake Junaluska.

Knowing Jesus From the Beginning

THE SALVATION ARMY · SOUTHERN TERRITORY · Bible Conference

August 11-18, 2013
Lake Junaluska, NC

In the morning Mia picked me up and we again headed to her community pool for another day of the Lord leading our conversation. Time flowed into the afternoon, and she decided our friendship had gotten to a point of bringing me to her home for dinner. Being handy on the grill, by late afternoon I was barbecuing while Mia stood knee-deep on the steps going into her pool. The scene was perfect. As we smiled at each other, I could not resist the temptation. I walked over, gently took her face in my hands, and planted one right on her lips, at which point I felt that same spiritual electricity as when our arms brushed at Bible study.

Greatly encouraged and hopeful to embrace this new level of relationship, right after the kiss I lost any remaining self-control to keep my and God's secret. I confessed my love to her and how the moment I saw her, God said "That's the one." This may not have been the best time to tell her—obviously desire for transparency and impulsive, human frailty took over. But we continued hanging out together into the evening, and though it appeared we were quite attracted to each other, we remained obedient to the Lord by *crucifying our flesh,* as Galatians 5:24 tells us to:

> *"Those who belong to Christ Jesus have crucified the flesh with its passions and desires."*

Back at ARC by 8pm, it was a tough night wrestling with whether I should have shared that much. I asked God's grace for my potentially hasty reveal after just one kiss, the sort of mistake Proverbs 17:28 warns about:

> *"Even fools are thought wise if they keep silent, and discerning if they hold their tongues."*

Too much information at the wrong time can drive people away, something Christians must keep in mind when witnessing to non-believers. From my extensive study of God's Word, these days life is exponentially clearer, but we can never stop growing in the knowledge of Jesus—the children of God will be discovering our Heavenly Father's mind for eternity. And through our learning process, God's grace comes in when we make juvenile mistakes. Being able to see our hearts in all matters, the Lord knows whether we're trying to do things righteously in His sight or acting from the wrong motivations.

I awoke early the next morning for my journey to North Carolina, but before I boarded the bus, Mia called to say she would be right over. I had left my *Baker Illustrated Bible* at her house, so she got up at 5am to bring it to me before the trip. She arrived as we were about to leave, gave me a big hug, said to have a great time, told me to call later so she knew I made it okay, and handed me a CD of excellent music from Christian artists she thought I would enjoy on the ride. With her going to all that trouble for this homeless guy, it appeared my premature disclosures had not sent her running for the exit, and she might even be open to God saying she's the one. Either way I was at peace knowing all was in God's hands; He would enlighten Mia in His own way.

10

"When Love Is Just Right!"

August 11th I was on the Salvation Army bus headed for North Carolina, a route that took us past Georgia exits for Valdosta and Lake Lanier, respectively the birthplaces of Mia (the one) and Michelle (the one that got away). Again, the two ladies could seriously pass for identical twins, and Michelle's last name is the same as the maiden name of Mia's grandmother. What are the odds that the two most significant women in my life would look like sisters, grow up a few hundred miles from each other, move south to the Tampa area, and end up dating me?

At one point on our trip, we decided to pop Mia's music into the bus's CD player, a mix she put together through guidance from the Holy Spirit. It would be the type of music that makes you want to close your eyes, lift your hands to God, and get lost in His presence. Unfortunately, the bus ate it. The CD would not play. So, we listened to the radio.

Just after we crossed the Florida state line, the Holy Spirit began prompting me to do something I had never done before: write poetry. Three days after that spiritual jolt of electricity from brushing Mia's arm, I felt the Holy Spirit was about to confirm through my writing that Mia's and my love was just right. Here is what He wrote through me:

When Love Is Just Right!

When love is right, you just know,
Especially when the Holy Spirit speaks to confirm it is so.
Trust in God; love Him, honor Him, and truly believe, Do
this justly and without reprieve.

He'll bless your soul and your heart's desire,
Then bring you someone destined to inspire,
Someone beautiful, gentle, and kind,
For this is truly a gift from heaven's most divine.

An angel of mercy, full of grace,
Who knows life is a journey and never a race.
A child of yours, Lord, holy and pure,
She's my strength, my pillar who holds me near.

True love, oh Lord, sent from above,
Filled with the Holy Spirit and peace of a dove.
Thank you my Savior, Lord, Teacher, and Friend,
My heart once broken, now begins to mend.

I'm sorry I doubted your power and might,
I now believe in love at first sight.
When we're together Lord, with her eyes so blue,
I see inside her a fire burning for You.

I know You have us Lord, my fear is no more,
Again, she's my Angel, on her wings I will soar.
As high as an eagle destined to reign,
With her beside me from Cali to Maine.

Doing Your work, oh Lord, until we grow old,
A biblical love story for others to behold.
Giving thanks and praise to You, Lord, each time I've kissed
her good night,
As this gives conviction to the phrase, "When Love is Just
Right!"

I wept while writing it and was excited to give the poem to Mia when I got back home from that week of miracles, signs, and wonders. One miraculous God-incident happened as I had just finished writing *and* we were passing the exit I used to take to Michelle's house—Mia's music CD began playing! I had started the poem on I-75 near the Valdosta, Georgia, exit where Mia was from, and finished a few hours later just before Michelle's Atlanta exit. Suddenly God's playlist came on!

Rocky and Jared (my Christian brothers who counseled me to be careful of finances and *romances* during rehab) were on the bus when that music suddenly came on *five hours* after putting it in the bus's dashboard, *as* I was finishing the poem, *and* right while passing Michelle's exit. I reminded them of my claim that Mia's and my relationship was the Lord's doing, not just some fleshly mistake. They were perplexed, especially knowing Mia and having also met Michelle when she visited four weeks earlier. So, on top of all that had just happened, they already knew the two women look similar. My friends' faces began to express some understanding of what God might be orchestrating with Mia and me.

Later that week Rocky and Jared would see God show up again. For whatever reason, I had told them how Mia saw a shooting star around the time she had been praying about whether to continue a relationship with me. She thought that might be a sign—but needed more confirmation. Then while confessing her thoughts concerning me to her neighbor (best friend Valerie), she saw a second shooting star. Although Mia thought it might mean God was orchestrating something greater, Valerie cautioned:

"Really, Mia? He's a homeless guy."

Now a couple weeks later in Maggie, North Carolina, here I was walking around with the ARC guys, shopping the tourist stores for family gifts. Suddenly, Rocky felt the Holy Spirit was leading us toward a certain store. He announced:

"I don't even know why, but we really need to look in here."

Right inside the door, I immediately looked left and saw a pair of *shooting-star* earrings. That was it. I truly believed this would be confirmation for Mia *and* the guys—the third shooting star! I let Rocky know this was why God prompted him to that store. The Lord was easing my Christian brother's concerns about Mia and me. God often confirms his Word to (and through) witnesses—especially doubting Thomases (John 20:27) who must see to believe. The Lord confirms His truth in mighty ways, often with miracles and wonders that even the most skeptical can't ignore. Fortunately, we were given $100 spending cash for this trip. I had just enough left to buy Mia her confirming stars. But would these earrings be enough?

Getting back to earlier in the week, we arrived at the retreat to beautiful hotel rooms overlooking majestic Lake Junaluska in front of the Great Smoky Mountains. Fortunately, my dear Christian brother Blake was also asked to attend as a way for the Salvation Army to say thank you for his service on the board of directors. Three and a half months after he had rescued me into the ARC program, he and I got to bunk together at this amazing place where the Salvation Army holds its annual Faith Convention, a function that brings in beneficiaries for a life-changing experience. They are chosen on merit from all over the eastern United

States. God sure enjoys showing off through the lives of those who stay obedient to His Word—to Him be the glory!

Although Blake and I are best friends, prior to this North Carolina trip I had not yet mentioned my flourishing relationship with Mia. He would soon find out when overhearing a call to Mia where I mentioned writing the poem—after never having done so before—and how it appeared to be the Lord giving her and me a relationship message. Blake had known me for twenty years and poetry was certainly never discussed between us, so after reading it to Mia, I could see that he understood I was not the author. Mia questioned whether this was really my first poetry. I said that maybe God was awakening a gift He had given me even before being in my mother's womb, and it would be interesting to see what writing He inspires next.

Blake was supportive right away, never questioning the Lord's power at work in Mia's and my relationship, and he especially got on board going forward as he would witness many more amazing "God incidents": signs, miracles, and wonders that follow Christians who are in close relationship with their Creator. A small but convincing one happened when I had to use Blake's smartphone—mine was an old flip phone—to receive a music video from Mia. We were standing outside the chapel where Oscar Roan was getting ready to preach a sermon. The song Mia sent was "We Were Made to Worship" by Chris Tomlin, and the video part involved a beautiful field of sunflowers, the exact sort surrounding that worship center we would soon walk into. In fact, we somewhat seriously wondered whether Tomlin had shot his music video in front of that chapel. This "coincidence" Blake got to see was just God's warmup for what you will read about in the rest of this book.

Once inside the chapel, our first speaker was Oscar Roan, a former NFL star running back in the 1970s. Like me, he had struggled with addiction (his included drugs *and* alcohol) until developing a personal relationship with Jesus. At seventy years old, he was still sharing Christ's gospel with those who need to know that Jesus makes *all* things possible. Oscar's first wife went to be with the Lord after a bout with cancer, and after some time being single, he had recently remarried. Before Oscar got into his message, I nearly fell out of my pew when he introduced his wife and beamed about knowing the moment, he met her that *she was the one* and how they *got married within six months!* I later told Mia about the comment and asked if she thought it coming at the start of our first sermon was maybe just a coincidence. She was hesitant to say so, but I could sense she was open to it being a sign.

I would share each day's notes with Mia, as the Lord kept drawing us closer to Him and each other. A couple times that week I again told Mia I loved her and that, no matter what would transpire going forward, God was doing something special between us. Our conversations became more intimate in the pure sense of steadily increasing affection for one another, and though feelings are not always facts, the relationship seemed to have me in the uncharted waters of falling in love *through Christ*. This was contrary to all my worldly relationships that quickly became physically intimate, after which we might move in together, with the idea of *potentially* marrying one day. But it would never happen. We always broke up. The end—again.

Monumentally different, Mia and I were completely surrendered to the will of God. Together on the phone each night, we prayed fervently for the Father to bless our relationship and help us remain obedient to His Word. I told Mia how the retreat presented many couples who had been married thirty to fifty years as Salvation Army officers, and each gave this recommendation:

"Put Christ first in your relationship and all will be well."

These were some of God's finest servants on the planet, people who had served the Lord for decades by helping the less fortunate find their way to the love of Christ. Thinking back on that week, I am so thankful the Lord had me hear from those wonderful, Holy Spirit-filled believers who lived joyful lives because their marriages were built around Jesus and serving others as He did. After sharing these testimonies with Mia, we both better understood why the Holy Spirit had me pen a poem about how God-centered relationships tend to find a love that is just right.

11

"What Is Love?"

Genesis was a focus of our talks during the retreat, leading this new believer to many revelations, like how the Old Testament—even from its first book—foreshadowed our Heavenly Father's master plan to redeem His fallen creation through sin-sacrifice, which later culminated in Him offering the death of Jesus, His only begotten Son. The scarlet thread of Christ became known to me through careful study of Genesis, something explained well here with quotations from Hebrews 9:22 mixed in:

> "Theologians and Bible students sometimes refer to 'the scarlet thread running through the Bible.' By this they mean that the Bible's theme is Jesus Christ and His sacrifice for the redemption of mankind. The blood of Christ runs throughout the entire Bible, symbolically.. . . 'Without the shedding of blood there is no forgiveness.' "[4]

We studied how the flood of Noah—a worldwidse deluge backed up by over 500 cultures that have history documenting a similar story—was Old Testament symbolism for how sinners were to put their faith in the coming Messiah, who turned out to be Jesus, as a personal ark of safety from ending up in hell because of sin. We also talked about how Abraham was willing to do whatever God wanted—even to the point of sacrificing his son Isaac—and how that was a foreshadow of the Heavenly Father asking His own Son to die on a cross for His Father's glory, all creation, and humanity's sins. Later in Mia's and my relationship, this same sort of selfless sacrifice was something I would live out through God's test of whether I would let Mia go. More on that later, but what I learned was that Genesis is the first of sixty-six books of the Bible that are God penning a

---

4 https://www.gotquestions.org/scarlet-thread.html

love story between Him and His children.

That first book of Scripture also uses the example of Adam and Eve to explain what the Lord means by marriage, something I and Mia wanted to exemplify in our God-centered relationship. In fact, I could see God's hand helping us become closer each night that week as we talked on the phone. At the same time the retreat involved so many Salvation-Army-officer couples who met, fell in love, and quickly married with Christ as their firm foundation. While experiencing a personal love story with Mia, I imagined Adam's excitement when he awoke to see Eve for the first time. At that moment, maybe God told Adam exactly what the Lord would also say to me 6000 years later: "That's the one." Did God mention love to the first couple? Did Adam and Eve have many questions about it? Did God teach them about sacrifice for the sake of others, including how a joyful life involves taking the focus off yourself and putting it on God, family, friends, and strangers in need?

On the trip back to Florida, the bus CD player worked perfectly. I sat in the back going through notes from the excellent teachings and reminiscing about the week's heartfelt conversations with Mia. While reminiscing about all God had revealed on marriage and obsessing over the definition of love, I began weeping when the Holy Spirit prompted me to write Mia another poem. At that time, I knew God was putting out the poetry and that He had chosen Mia for me, but it appeared He was perfecting a method to tell Mia that I am the one for her. With that in mind, on August 18th, 2013, the Holy Spirit seemed to be offering Mia more evidence written through my hand. A question-and-answer poem perhaps? Well, you decide:

What Is Love?

Oh those days we sit and ponder the question. . . What is love?
Well. . .the answer is divine. . .sent from heaven above.
Look at this man's heart once made of stone,
no longer beating lost and all alone!

Just lift your eyes to heaven and open your soul,
Feel the glory of God when His love begins to flow.
Feel the peace and serenity as the turbulent sea calms,
Like the warmth of a sunset seen through the leaves of palms.

Now, as the day becomes night. . .do not worry,
For His love still shines bright and will never scurry.

Look at the stars so far away,
Beautiful, majestic, and in the heavens they will stay.

Ah. . . What is love? Need you ask more?
It's right in front of you. . . Just open the door.
Walk through, humbled and without fear,
Feel the Holy Spirit with a smile and a tear.

You've been touched by love, holy and clean,
My God, my Savior. . . His wonders yet to be seen.
For me it's an angel with wings of gold,
One with eyes of blue and a spirit that is bold.

Two become one in the eyes of the Lord,
*We're **better together** with the Bible as our sword.*
The enemy has no chance in our house of bricks,
we've both been lost and know all of his tricks.

Destined to save lives in the name of Christ,
We know we're different, blessed, and convicted. . .never
thinking twice!
I no longer question. . . What is love?
I found someone to walk with. . .sent from heaven above.

My heart no longer empty and hard as that stone,
Full of the Holy Spirit and no longer alone.
Dropping to our knees each night before bed,
To give thanks and praise before we lay down our heads.

Drifting off to sleep now together as one,
Hearts and souls mended by Jesus, God's Son.
So, let's stop questioning. . . What is love?
Just lift your eyes to heaven above.

Not long after I wrote this poem that twice mentions my former heart of stone, Mia was sitting in the grass where she would often study. There she was talking to God about our new relationship, when she put her hand down on a small piece of the foundation that had broken off from her fifteen-year-old home. Looking at it, she noticed the rock was in the shape of a heart—and looked like it had a cross etched on it. Was this a sign connected to my references about having a heart of stone?

Rereading those words today, I am aware that one reason the Holy Spirit penned them through me was to show how God can use any person to deliver His message. You may recall that I had arrogantly and naively challenged Christianity by claiming the Lord did not need—and would not use—humans to write for Him. What an amazing testimonial to God's glory that (from before birth) He gave that same previously deceived man some sort of poetry gift that would end up countering my prior deceived assertions. And though the words of that poem were not my own, God blessed me to witness the effect they had on Mia, something I will get to in a minute.

Arriving back home in Tampa was bittersweet. I would be able to see Mia, but the week had included eight- to twelve-hour days of life-changing sermons, a luxurious hotel room, the majestic view, excellent fellowship meals, and an incredible gym with the best equipment (something I can attest to as a former bodybuilder). Unlike the ARC program, there was no waking up at 5am, using a community bathroom, and having to shower with a hundred men. For a week in North Carolina, I had tasted the fruit of living a life honorable to God, whose favor had clearly been on me to even go on that retreat: out of 150 guys possible, only I and four others were chosen. Also returning to my days would be the hard work that paid room and board in the ARC program, an understandable requirement but another reason it was hard returning to the reality of "Sally living" (Salvation Army life).

Fortunately, we made it back early enough that I could spend a few evening hours with Mia, so we sat and read the new poem. Once finished, with tearful eyes she asked:

*"Are you **sure** you had never written poetry?"*

I replied that I too was surprised. We hugged intensely. Even cried some. We were both overwhelmed to witness how God brings a man and woman together in a loving relationship centered on Him, one that demonstrates what love is by creating a love that is just right.

"What Is Love?"

12

"Where Are We Now?"

It was not long before Mia would confess to caring deeply for me. I could sense truth in her voice and knew the Holy Spirit had been working on her heart—some of which included the poems He penned through me. We would talk every afternoon, and a couple nights each week she would pick me up to get coffee or just sit in a nearby parking lot where we would do divine flips (randomly flipping through the Bible). Though the practice is not something we still do or would recommend, Mia and I landed on many passages that brought up heartfelt conversations relating to where we were in our relationship with God and each other; after all, God gave mankind the Bible as our instruction book for life. The vast majority of non-believers wonder who we humans are, how we ended up here on earth, and what our purpose is. With no answers—or false ones—many agonize their entire lives from a lack of hope for the future. But that need not be: God generously supplies all that information in His easy-to-understand Bible. The founder of the Biblical Research Society, Dr. David L. Cooper (1886–1965), said this:

> *"When the plain sense of Scripture makes common sense, seek no other sense. . .unless the facts of the immediate context. . .indicate clearly otherwise."*

And because Christians know that God's Word gives a simple explanation of every person's purpose in life, we believers must help the Lord inform unbelievers. God blesses us to be an eternity-altering blessing to those who still have a Jesus-size hole in their hearts.

As Mia and I spent more time together, our mutual affection grew by leaps and bounds. We regularly attended Bible study on Thursday nights, as well as church on Saturday nights and Sunday mornings.

There were conversations about marriage, but little of it serious except for our agreement that we would do it God's way, not even entertaining the idea of living together first. And we were not interested in a drawn-out engagement: we recognized that the Lord had us meet many godly couples who married within six months of dating. Was he asking us to do the same? One Saturday night as we prepared for church at Grace Family, Mia decided to wear her high heel shoes, meaning she was going to tower over me again. So, I jokingly said:

"Okay, I'll be your David if you be my Goliath."

Little did I know, Assistant Pastor Dean's sermon that night would be about those two Bible characters. He spoke about unmeasurable faith and demonstrated the concept by recalling how he had met his wife, knew through faith that *she was the one,* and they *were married within six months*—I almost fell out of my chair this time. Mia missed it since she had to attend her prayer team meeting, so I told her and she picked up the sermon CD for her ride toward St. Augustine (on Florida's northeast coast) that night, a trip to visit her brother at Crescent Beach. Once she had also heard what Pastor Dean said, she commented about it being the second time we had heard pastors say they got married within six months of meeting their wives. Then she added something that would have a lot of significance going forward in our relationship with God and each other:

"God always confirms things in threes, so I need to hear it one more time before I can believe it's what the Lord has in store for us."

Mia was still quite skeptical that this homeless guy might be her knight in shining armor. Like any somewhat wise man dating a woman, I agreed with her statement, especially since my opinion would have made no difference to her belief. Besides, God had already told me. He needed to show her. The next morning, He did. After I attended another Salvation Army church service like the one where I got saved, Mia called and could barely contain her excitement enough to tell me what happened. While staying at her brother's house, she enjoyed getting up before the sun and walking across the street to the beach where she can see it come up. From her description and pictures, the beautiful sunrise that morning was accompanied by calm weather, crystal clear water, and a comfortable temperature.

But this time something strange happened: while she watched the sky, a gentleman who was also taking in the sunrise suddenly appeared next to her. She said their conversation somehow quickly went to supernatural topics, like how people sometimes have premonitions that become true. Remember, Mia had dabbled in New Age. And her draw to that false-spirit movement was from her *God*-given gifts that *the enemy* was trying to hijack for his purposes and pleasure. Mia's ability to discern spirits and prophetically know things were talents meant to bring God glory (again, please see the New Age addendum at the back of this book).

This gentleman also said he did not believe in coincidences, so there must be a reason he and she were talking. Agreeing with that, Mia thought it might be appropriate to share with him the Bible devotional she had been reading. Once finished, he shocked Mia to her core with something he said he felt led to tell her:

"I knew my wife was the one when I first met her, so within six months we were married."

Suddenly beside herself, she declared:

"That's why you're here!"

Then after turning back to the sunrise for a moment to ponder the magnitude of that third confirmation, Mia glanced back his way, but the man was gone—completely. He disappeared. To this day we are convinced he had been Mia's "angel unaware": she was entertaining an angel, something Hebrew 13:2 informs us about:

> *"Be not forgetful to entertain strangers: for thereby some have entertained angels unawares."*

God had already told me about His plans for us, and now this incident helped Mia see how He was orchestrating our relationship, something she needed because her perception of us was surely being influenced by the idea that a homeless, jobless, penniless guy might be hunting for an established woman he can cling to. The world's norm is "boy meets girl, takes girl out, pays attention to girl, compliments girl, and showers girl with gifts, thus establishing his image as a desirable, successful, well-rounded provider." These can even be the sorts of honorable attributes a Christian woman wants in the man of her dreams.

That said, what if she meets a destitute man who lives with a new fire and passion for Christ that will likely lead him to become that sort of provider? In my situation as Mia and I began to date, the world would have been surprised at my confidence as potential husband material. But God was supernaturally giving me strength and hope from my willingness to surrender each day to Him, walking in His ways and letting Him take care of the rest. My *only* concern was remaining obedient to God's Word, which allowed Mia to see Christ in me, creating a peaceful courtship, rather than me having to labor under low self-esteem from a lack of worldly success at that time.

Our relationship was feeling just right, and God was showing up everywhere we went. In fact, one evening, a week after Mia had her angelic *sunrise* encounter at Crescent Beach, she and I sat on Clearwater Beach, waiting for what would be a beautiful *sunset* over the Gulf of Mexico. While talking about how grateful we were that the Lord had been speaking to us so often, we glanced down the beach to where a man was walking the shoreline, carrying a twelve-foot cross. We instantly knew God had placed us there to see him, so we walked to the water's edge and spoke to Ed, who attends a local church and "carries" out his ministry all over the United States—he is a true brother in Christ.

Although most everything felt right about our relationship, I struggled from being homeless with no income. Having been an entrepreneur on a six-figure income, it was difficult to feel like I was displaying a God-honoring example of the Christian life: I could not pick her up, pay for dinner and a movie, or even buy her a small popcorn. Worse still, Mia had to cover my expenses for everything we did, and she had the added burden of explaining our relationship to her friends who were concerned about her dating a rehabbing, homeless addict. Other doubts I had involved Mia's belief that her ex-husband might still be who God intended for her. Maybe their marriage only initially failed because she and he were not following the Word of the Lord. Knowing Mia's obedient heart for God—her wanting to be a godly wife and mother—I knew reconciliation with him would be hard for her to walk away from.

During the next several weeks we remained emotionally close, but there seemed to be some sort of distance growing between us, so I leaned into the Holy Spirit for guidance, and He revealed that "my future wife" was slipping away. My spirit knew she needed closure: Mia had always been honest with me, mentioning that marriage reconciliation could possibly be part of God's plan, and if it was His will, she had to be willing. All this had me feeling like something was seriously amiss between Mia and me. The culmination of my angst came on the evening of September 23rd when I made the most difficult decision of my life, resulting in me calling Mia and sincerely offering her an open door out of our relationship, *if* that is what she thought best. Here is what I said to Mia when volunteering to walk away and let the Lord put them back together:

"The Spirit pressed it upon my heart to let you know it's okay to try again with Martin, and until you do so, we should not see each other. I want to be in the center of God's will with our relationship, and that means we can't move forward until you have closure."

Can you imagine me telling the woman I love—who I knew was God's choice for my wife—that she has my blessing to reconciled with her ex? But would you think it was the right decision if the Holy Spirit told me to? Well, He did. The Spirit spoke, declaring:

"You must be willing to let her go and be reconciled with her ex-husband, as this is what your Heavenly Father wants."

When I called to share God's message with Mia, she wept almost uncontrollably, but was also grateful that I felt the same as her. She had not wanted to tell me, but she knew our relationship was over—at least, until she could get closure. Hanging up the phone was hard.

As was becoming a Holy Ghostwriting custom, a collaboration of me and the Lord, strong emotions again caused me to race back to my room, pick up a pen, and put down this poem the Spirit had running through my head:

Where Are We Now?

I wondered if this relationship would end somehow,
Love was fleeting as I cried out to God, "Where Are We Now?"
I did not understand what was transpiring, as I was sure
this was fate,
But now I'm wondering if we will ever again date.

Upon miracles, signs, wonders, and a Voice from above,
The Lord showed me—then told me—this was the one I would love.
Fast and furious our love was ablaze,
Inspired by God these past forty-nine days.

But where are we now, for my soul yearns to know,
So much uncertainty, Lord, where should we go?
Turning to Your word in search of the truth,
Seeking Your Wisdom for a relationship still in its youth.

Lo and behold, Your word came alive,
As I turned to Second Corinthians, chapter ten, verses three
through five.
With our love now doomed and possibly dead,
Quickly I turned to 2 Corinthians 10: 3–5; this is what it said:

"For though we walk in the flesh, we do not war according to
the flesh. For the weapons of our warfare are not carnal but
mighty in God for pulling down strongholds, casting down
arguments and every high thing that exalts itself against the
knowledge of God, bringing every thought into captivity to
the obedience of Christ."

So, where are we now, from Your word as it is written;
Will our love continue to flourish, or, sadly, be smitten?
It was time to stand on faith and Your written word,
Knowing our love can't be broken, and to think so...is
undeniably absurd.

You showed me "the one," Lord, and You cannot lie,
A promise you made me for which You will not deny!
Remembering always...the enemy plays in our minds,
A battlefield of twisted thoughts only Christ can unwind.

Staying obedient to the Scriptures above,
I surrendered those strongholds to Christ and did so with love.
Trusting in You, Lord, without fear or doubt,
Yoking our hearts with Yours, where love never runs out.

These words poetically written for others to behold,
Words inspired by You, Lord, as Your truth must be told.
Our victory chapter complete, and these strongholds are no
more, Surrendered to Your Word as You open the next door.

*We'll step through **together**, as You show us the way,*
Praying Your will—not ours—be accomplished each day.
We're so grateful Lord, as You showed us somehow,
Answering the question "Where Are We Now?"

Again, the ability to write poetry was not something I have ever had or learned. Like the other two poems, this one was inspired by the Holy Spirit.

I knew in my heart that God does not lie, so when He said, "That's the one," at the moment I first laid eyes on Mia, it meant our marriage *would* come to pass. But as I learned later, before she and I were to end up together, the Lord was making her my "Isaac." You probably know the story. God promised to give a very old and childless couple, Abraham and Sarah, a son whose descendants would become great nations and include kings, and all families of the earth would be blessed through what Abraham would become patriarch of.

In fact, one of his descendants ended up being Jesus, who went on to save the fallen world from all being thrown in hell because we willingly sin. Sin is something the devil invented. Along with all humans to follow, even the first man and woman joined Satan in sin, so the initial Adam fell. But then the "last Adam"—our Messiah and Savior, Christ—arrived to redeem every sinful human who will humble themselves enough to call on Jesus's name for forgiveness of their sins.

Getting back to Abraham, it was crucially important that God be able to trust the potential father of an uncountable multitude with all that blessing. So, Abraham had to be willing to sacrifice everything, even his and Sarah's only son, if that was what God required. Abraham complied with his Heavenly Father's wishes, tied Isaac up on a sacrifice altar, and raised his knife to kill the young man. But the Lord stopped him. Abraham passed the test. God spared Isaac.

And now this sort of test was just what the same God of love and truth was asking of me. Was I willing to do whatever the Lord asked? Could He trust me to stay true to Him through any adversity? That might mean letting Mia go—the person I love more than anyone but Him—while also trusting God to somehow still fulfill the promise He showed earlier that Mia is the one I would marry.

Looking back, that was my most difficult decision so far as a Christian, an act of self-denial that would show the Lord how much my heart burns for His, ahead of *all* else. As with every human challenge, Scripture helped me through, specifically Romans 15:4 and Hebrews 11:1:

> *"For everything that was written in the past was written to teach us, so that through the endurance taught in the Scriptures and the encouragement they provide, we might have* **hope.***"*

> *"Now faith is confidence in what we* **hope** *for and assurance about what we do not see."*

There is *always* hope!

13

"Resting in His Promise Through the Storm"

So, I had hope, and my situation was expected: the Bible warns Christians that we cannot please God without faith, so it is something He gauges during life's inevitable trials and tribulations. Regardless, the next morning I became sick to my stomach. I could not resist doubts and still questioned God about why He would take away the one He promised. I wonder if Abraham too faced the same sorts of mind-corrupting doubts as he pushed through the trauma. He may have gotten the same divine message some other way, but like me he could have benefited from 2 Corinthians 10:5:

"Take captive every thought to make it obedient to Christ."

Though that's a New Testament reference for an Old Testament Abraham, the Word says Jesus existed before all things, so Abraham's test would have included whether he had faith in the coming Messiah (Who ended up being Jesus). Did he have doubts? I certainly did. That's the truth. But even during my brief walk with God, I had seen many of His signs, miracles, and wonders, so my heart knew God does the impossible.

Abraham (our father of the faith) did not deny or even question the Lord when asked to end Isaac's life. He kept faith throughout and that probably would have continued even if God had let Abraham's knife strike Isaac. The Lord would not have allowed Abraham's promised one to die without bringing him back to life. Likewise, knowing that Mia was the promised one who God told me about, I retained some peace from that divine promise.

Biblical history tells us that Abraham took Isaac up on the mountain, tied the young man to a sacrificial altar, and was obediently ready to run his knife through Isaac. But before he could, the "The angel of the Lord" commanded him to stop. The test was over. Abraham passed. Isaac lived. And Genesis 22:12–14 details what miraculously happened after that:

> *"Abraham looked up and there in a thicket he saw a ram caught by its horns. He went over and took the ram and sacrificed it as a burnt offering instead of his son. So Abraham called that place The Lord Will Provide. And to this day it is said, 'On the mountain of the Lord it will be provided.'"*

We include this Scripture to show how my and Mia's history tells more of God's story. From our study of His Word, we know our journey had parallels to events in the Bible, so this book is meant to help readers search for and recognize how their own paths have correlated with biblical truths. Abraham knew God had supernaturally provided the ram as a substitute sacrifice for Isaac, and we too can take comfort that He will always deliver on His promises to us by providing a way out—even when we fallible, fallen humans have lost all hope because the worst looks inevitable. God comforts us with the knowledge that we can pass any of His tests by remaining obedient to His commands.

A further demonstration of God's graciousness and miraculous power happened six months into my stay at the Salvation Army's ARC program. My main job was putting price tags on clothing to be sold at their thrift stores throughout Tampa's Hillsborough County. Those sales support their Christian rehabilitation ministries, and the whole process—which can take a couple months—starts with the public's donation of used items like clothes, dishes, furniture, televisions, bicycles, and even cars.

Imagine a day of spring cleaning when you finally finish going through old clothes and settle on what you'll donate. You pack up boxes or bags of your discards and drive them to some parking lot where you've seen a Salvation Army semitrailer. There the attendant takes your donation, thanks you for your kindness, and hands you a tax-donation receipt. Later in the evening a semi driver picks the trailer up and brings it to the Salvation Army ARC warehouse. If the trailer is not full, it will often be returned to the same attendant the following morning, and the process of filling it continues. When the trailer is eventually full, it gets emptied at the warehouse, where beneficiaries work for room and board over their six months of rehabilitation. From there the trailer loads are sorted by type of donation. Clothes are put into bins that are gone through to find items worthy of being sold at the stores. Then someone puts those on hangers and places them on racks of 125 to 150 pieces. Once full, a rack is rolled into the type of section where I worked at tagging them each with a price.

Daily countywide volume in a city like Tampa is massive, so six days per week about twenty people are needed just to hang clothes on racks—ten more to pop on price tags. I alone would handle twenty to thirty racks each day. Around 25,000 pieces of clothing per day were prepared for either the thrift stores or overseas missions.

On a normal day of clothes-tagging, we faced an endless parade of racks, but the stress was exponentially higher the morning after giving my blessing for the woman I love to reconcile with her ex-husband. Still, I reported for duty with price gun in hand, understanding that the work must continue, and I needed to do my part. Adding to my heavy heart was the fact that Mia and her ex would be meeting for lunch to talk about reconciliation. To her boys, Mia had promised that the next guy she dated would be the one she marries; she would never again be a casually dating, worldly sort of woman. She also knew God's character includes His will for restoration. She cared deeply for me and knew God was in the middle of her and my relationship, but also that this closure had to take place if we were to continue.

Knowing that, I stayed in constant dialogue with my Heavenly Father, going over and over all that transpired the previous night, and praying for clarification as to why He would bring Mia into my life and then ask me to give her up. My mind raced, but prayer provided a bit of peace. As God probably did for Abraham in the midst of his mental storm, the Lord was giving me a feeling that everything would be all right in the end. My faith knew God would at least produce reassurance that He was in control of it all. Unfortunately for future thrift-store shoppers though, my absentmindedness that day surely created tags with a few crazy bargains, as well as some very expensive used clothes.

I admire how the Salvation Army throws away all T-shirts that depict sex, drugs, alcohol, or anything contrary to God's Word. What makes it to me has mostly uplifting slogans or Scripture passages, which help with a monotonous eight hours. Near 1pm, I asked God to give me a sign about what was happening at Mia's lunch meeting; I was waiting on Him to show me His planned way out of the situation. While still praying for clarity, I smiled as a familiar *I Love You* shirt came through, with a large red heart replacing *Love*.

Three shirts later, while still smiling from my belief that God had sent me a love message in the midst of my storm, I nearly dropped my tagging gun when the next one was from a company formerly owned by Mia's ex-husband—the print included his last name! It was as if the Holy Spirit was letting me know He understands my situation, loves me, and has this whole reconciliation lunch under control. Like the ram supplied to Abraham, God was showing me that He would provide a way out of my agonizing situation. And He did: because of her ex's current relationship, he had no intentions of reconciliation, giving Mia the peace she needed to close that chapter of her life.

As far as how that shirt miraculously showed up on my rack, Mia had donated it three months earlier. She dropped it off with other clothes at a Salvation Army trailer. Because that branch of her ex's company had dissolved a few years prior, there were not many of those shirts around. I had not seen one in five months, probably because it was put out several years earlier in a very limited production. With a daily mountain of 25,000 pieces going through ten taggers, what are the odds of it coming to me on that day three months later, around the exact time Mia was finishing lunch, and as I was asking God to show me the way that would lead to fulfillment of His promise that Mia is the one.

Jesus fulfilled over 300 specific Old Testament prophecies. The chances of all that being a coincidence are the same odds as me successfully throwing a baseball to the moon—or that shirt showing up at the exact time and place it did. Like Abraham's sacrificial ram supernaturally appearing with its horns caught for easy capture, God also answered my prayers by letting me see His miraculous power. Abraham assured Isaac that God would provide—and He did—just as the Holy Spirit comforted me that day at a Salvation Army warehouse.

When your faith is put to the ultimate test, I pray you stand strong on His Word and rest in His promises, recognizing that God will provide a way out.

14

"Slow Progress Through Perseverance"

Though Mia and I made it through that painful time, our relationship was still far from the point of living happily ever after. We had witnessed God's miraculous power to restore hope, but I was still a homeless Salvation Army beneficiary living under the rules and regulations I had agreed to five and a half months earlier. With only two weeks until graduation, gainful employment was not even on my horizon. I wanted to finish recovery, jump back into the game of life, and finally be able to take Mia on dates.

For three months she had hung in to support me and was rewarded with much evidence of God working in our relationship. So, Mia was also coming to realize that she might be the one. Like financial security gained by slow and steady investment over time, it seemed Mia was willing to have the patience needed and put in the extended efforts required for our relationship to grow. Proverbs 13:11 talks about the lasting rewards that can only be gained through persistent diligence over time:

> *"Dishonest money dwindles away, but whoever gathers money little by little makes it grow."*

Mia was hanging in there with me to witness a man transforming from decades of worldly living to a life worth living. God was molding obedient Robby into someone He could better use to advance His kingdom. Like Mia's perseverance in our relationship, I had been steadily progressing in rehabilitation, and my ARC graduation finally arrived on October 15th, 2013. Of those who begin the ARC program, only a small percentage finish, so the Salvation Army hands out a certificate of completion as part of an elaborate ceremony attended by those who supported the beneficiary for the previous six months. Graduates are even given three minutes of microphone time. I was honored to have Mia and our entire church family witness mine. Afterward they showered me with gifts for the achievement. Still near and dear today is a present from my pastor: *Sparkling Gems*, a daily devotional by Rick Renner. The book gives Scripture's Greek translations and in-depth commentaries that combine to reveal the full breadth of God's Word.

During those first three months dating Mia, I had been transparent to all who would listen about my faith, recovery, and relationship with her. But I was still learning Mia's approach. Though she and I were both recovering addicts, on fire for the Lord, and ready to help anyone who wanted to be set free from addiction, Mia was much more private about her personal life. She is bold as a lion when it comes to professing Jesus, but when prompted to speak, she waits to be led by the Holy Spirit. I eagerly jump at opportunities to share the good news of salvation through Christ, impulsively telling those around me how much Jesus loves them. Neither method is wrong. We're just different. Two approaches.

God has a way of pairing flawed people—especially a man and woman—who can help each other overcome unique struggles so the two can accomplish more of His will and be *better together*. I knew the godly union of Mia and me was the Lord's plan, but only six months into my life with Christ, I was still *deeply* flawed and often overstepped my bounds in the relationship. For example, during my graduation speech I was led to share one of the poems I wrote Mia; I wanted everyone to know how much I loved her. But looking back, it would have made sense to consider her privacy and consult her about how much of our relationship would be appropriate to reveal in public. Even today I often struggle at bridling my tongue, not considering other people's feeling enough and instead blurting out too much truth. Even with God's help, the magnitude of my life changes meant slow progress through perseverance in many areas of who I was.

From her faith in Christ, Mia granted me grace and mercy for my ignorance, but looking back at the ceremony pictures, you can see her displeased disposition. Though she was supportive and proud of my accomplishment, I could still sense a distance between us, including her having reservations about whether she could trust me to guard certain details of our relationship. We had become best friends, so it was easy to notice her negative emotions. I could also sense her disappointment that I was graduating without a post-rehab plan. These were not easy times.

She was anxious for me to figure out my future serving God, but because relationships are complicated, she also cautioned me not to move too fast. Mia wanted me to step up and be the man of her dreams, but to do so maturely. She was much more biblically seasoned than I.

Mia understood that I was eager to hit corporate America again and earn the type of windfall that would amaze her, the sort of success our world appreciates. But the last thing she wanted was our desires for my success to interfere with God's plan for my future. The Lord had been blessing my life through my best friend Mia's biblically educated wisdom, and this time was no different: she knew not to get ahead of God, while I was focused on dazzling my girl by hopping on the hamster wheel. Forget the homeless dude. I'll impress her. Watch me climb!

But neither Mia nor God was looking for this newly on-fire Christian to pursue a quick corporate ascension. Mia would have no part of it, and I ended up grateful. Instead of impressing her, she impressed upon me the importance of waiting on divine direction, something I still find easier said than done.

The Salvation Army prescribes six months for graduating their recovery program, but they know it may not be sufficient time for a beneficiary to fully and safely transition back into the world. So, I was allowed to stay up to half a year longer, if I would continue earning room and board by working for them. Like all beneficiaries during that extended time, I had a counselor who helped me get ready for the coming transition back into society. His name was Tommy Craig, and he was such a blessing, a strong Christian and completely supportive of my relationship with Mia— the Holy Spirit had showed him that God brought about our union.

Tommy helped throughout and especially when I felt Mia slipping further and further away. As she tried to adjust to my unique situation, Mia faced doubt and fear about an unknown future, wrestling with her desire to be a protective mother and with her previous marriage. I sensed her getting outside pressure from friends and family who wanted her to think hard about where our relationship could go. Those challenging Mia were looking out for her best interests, and today I consider many of them my brothers and sisters—who I love very much. But that doubt was the perfect opportunity for the enemy to infiltrate Mia's thoughts and try to extinguish our godly relationship before it could get more spiritually powerful against him and his demons.

My faith was again being tested as I sat at the Salvation Army waiting on God's instruction. My heartfelt questions were about why He had not yet opened a door for me to move forward in His plan—one that would also impress the woman He chose for me—and why He had been showing us so many godly couples who met, knew God put them together, and married within six months. One example came from what seemed like an angel God sent Mia at sunrise on Crescent Beach.

But I could not afford to get married anytime soon, so this flawed man was seeking answers, as God was again testing whether I would trust Him and His timing or take matters into my own hands. Of course, the latter would lead to horrible witnessing for God while professing Him, which would likely end up turning people off to Christianity. Instead, the Lord was showing me more about slow progress through perseverance.

As Thanksgiving approached, together Mia and I continued attending Thursday night Bible study and weekend church services. Since she was part of Grace Family's team that is available to pray with people after services, we went to church Saturday nights and Sunday mornings. So, the surface of our relationship seemed fine, but it was faltering. Though we were both spiritually seeking God and spending much time in His Word, our union was stagnating, mainly because I continued living at the Salvation Army with no plans to move out and get a real job anytime soon. Mia had encouraged me to be patient, but enough was enough already! The pressure mounted and fear was creeping back in, as I think it was for Mia. I was having an intimate relationship with Christ while still pursuing some of the world's ideas about right, wrong, and success.

With an addiction-free holiday season approaching, I began to panic about what I might buy Mia with my weekly $25 allowance from the Salvation Army. No job meant no gifts. What should I do? What could I do? As a dating couple, we generally ate out a couple times each week—and she paid for everything. Other than what we get through a relationship with God, men's self-esteem tends to depend on what we are achieving in the world, and here I was a kept man by Mia, as well as by my temporary boarding house. I could imagine what Mia must have been thinking, and it severely bothered me. I was not assuming the man's godly leadership role in a Christian relationship, or even the secular world's traditional way a gentleman pays on dates, and Mia was not accustomed to being a sugar mama.

Approaching four months with Mia, she was still reluctant to bring me around her home when her two boys were there. In fact, I hadn't even officially met them, most likely because she was protecting them and me. But Mia's ex-husband decided to attend Grace Family with their boys on a Saturday night, so I would finally meet them, after we three agreed to introduce me as a friend. If Mia and I ended up working out, I would not be a total stranger to the boys, and they could learn that she and I had become more than friends. I'm sure Mia had been praying that I would be back on my feet by this point: me being established would help her ex and the boys feel confident that she was with a stable guy. Though I was not some random, destitute idiot and didn't want to care about other people's perceptions, I could see my circumstance in the world's eyes—and I did not like it. It felt terrible. So, I worried.

On a positive note, her boys were two of the politest young men a mother could ask for, and I immediately hit it off with her ex-husband. I could see he was a great father and also supportive of what Mia was doing with her life.

Another significant part of that November was Mia attending a class at Life Christian University. She had a textbook titled *The Minister's Life of Obedience,* by Dr. Phillip Gary Richards, and she even grabbed a second copy so we could read it together; after all, God said we would be doing ministry together. Mia also surprised me with a ticket to see the Christian band Hillsong. I was so excited to go but had to back out when the Salvation Army denied my request to attend. They had invited a special guest preacher for the weekend, and those sorts of events were not something beneficiaries could miss.

Because Mia has many Christian friends, she easily found someone to go last minute. But the denial caused me deep resentment toward my benefactors for not letting me go—honestly, I acted out like a spurned child whose mom denies him candy at the grocery, so he screams and rolls around on the floor. I even took my case to the top brass, questioning why a graduate could not attend an outside Christian event. The unsatisfying answer was that it's the rule, they were not going to make an exception, and the only way for me to go was by packing my things and moving out.

Would God prepare someone for ministry with a lesson like that? Yes. He was teaching me about pride versus humility. And maybe I needed to hear the preacher more than a concert. As you may have guessed, the message they made me attend was much needed: he talked about how God seeks the keys to every door of the human heart, so you and I must surrender all those keys to His authority, fully handing over our hearts to Him. The Lord knows us best, the fruits of the Spirit—love, peace, joy, patience, etc.—flow from Him, and all He requires is for believers to let go of attitudes like selfishness that can block a more intimate relationship with Him.

God confirmed that teaching at the following Thursday night Bible study when our pastor's wife delivered almost the exact same message. . .while looking at me. I fell to my knees and wept, repenting for my reluctance to give God my whole heart. I was still holding certain keys from Him, so God would not be able to reach attitudes I wanted to hold onto like selfishness. Christians tend to take areas of our will back from the Lord— not His will, but ours.

Because of my overly negative response to the Hillsong disappointment, Mia pulled back even further. We spoke little before she left to spend Thanksgiving week in the North Carolina mountains with her children and former mother-in-law. Mia said it might be a helpful opportunity for us to take time away from each other and not speak, adding that she needed to reevaluate our relationship and give me time to get alone with God, seeking His direction for the relationship and my future career path. Again, displaying the ways of a fallen man, I fell back into doubting what God revealed about Mia and me, bringing on another long heart-to-heart with my Lord. I asked what He wanted from me before He would reveal how Mia and I were going to become man and wife. The Lord let me know I must continue working on patience, obedience, trust, and repentance.

After prayer to rectify my lack of those traits, and before Mia left, I called her to apologize for my ungodly, childish behavior. She listened with compassion and let me know she needed some days of prayer to seek God's will for what she was feeling. Like always, we were leaving it in His hands.

While Mia was gone, I dove deeply into *The Minister's Life of Obedience*, a powerful, awe-inspiring book that helped me better understand obedience to my Heavenly Father, hearing and obeying Him—no matter the cost. The book rekindled my fire to pursue the purposes for which I was created and to do so in patience and obedience. I knew that if only I would be obedient to His commands and fully trust the path God had me on, He would bring His promises to my life. I needed to wait on slow progress through godly perseverance.

When Mia and I were both about halfway through the book, she reached out to me from North Carolina. Our conversation was one of gracious forgiveness and about her also recognizing our future together; after all, God had shown her early on that we would do ministry together, helping set addiction captives free. We each related to the book's mention of Isaiah 6:8, a passage where the Lord questions Isaiah:

"Whom shall I send? Who will go for us?"

Isaiah obediently responded:

"Here I am. Send me!"

God knew the book by Dr. Richards was exactly what we both needed during this part of our walk with each other and Christ. To fully serve God, we must live a life of obedience. When I realized this, Mia's time in North Carolina did not turn out to be some prolonged time of distancing; instead, God blessed us with incredible conversations about rededication to our calling—no longer focused on negativity. After this attitude adjustment, our conversations during the latter half of Mia's time in North Carolina turned from the strife caused by my selfish pride to again celebrating the joy of our Lord. When we focused on what Jesus was doing and stopped dwelling on fears and selfishness, Mia's and my peace were restored. Clearing another hurdle helped us grow stronger as a Christian couple—praise God!

Though progress in our relationship had been slow, we were persevering, so the Lord showed up in amazing ways the rest of that week apart, like when Mia was led by the Holy Spirit to venture off the beaten path. She stopped in front of a closed restaurant that had hundreds of articles posted outside on the windows. There the Holy Spirit led her to look at Pastor John Hagee's article about blood moons, something Mia knew nothing about, but she was prompted to take note. Then her sharing this revelation with me ignited a fire in me to dig deeper. In fact, the first of those four blood moons would fall on April 15, my one-year anniversary of being clean and sober, a day that led to the Lord having me pen another poem.

That discovery and subsequent research on blood moons became an example of how Mia and I started more and more flowing together through God's revelations: still today, one of us will get a revelation from the Lord and then the Holy Spirit prompts the other to dig deeper into Scripture and the viewpoints of well-respected theologians and evangelists.

15

"God's Timing"

Though the enemy was trying to drive us apart with relationship strife, Mia's North Carolina trip was the second time those sorts of struggles ended up bringing us nearer to Christ and each other. By this point, we both had developed an in-depth understanding of God's ways versus the devils, and it led us to being skeptical of coincidences. Instead, we were more and more recognizing and embracing the signs, miracles, and wonders that occur—during peaks or valleys—when lives are lived on God's path. We were learning reliance on the Holy Spirit to teach us through Scripture.

Two trips to the mountains of North Carolina, mine and then Mia's, strengthened our relationship with God and each other. Higher elevations seem to foster closer communion with the Lord. I came back from Lake Junaluska floating on a cloud, and Mia's trip helped her clarify both individual and relationship purposes. I can see why Billy Graham settled in the mountains of North Carolina, living out the rest of his life in those amazing surroundings—before the exponentially better housing upgrade he now enjoys in heaven. As Paul tells us in Philippians 1:21:

> *"To live is Christ and to die is gain. . ."*

Our relationship was back on track, but gainful employment still wasn't on the horizon for me. With Christmas approaching, I knew a nice present for Mia would take a miracle, something I was getting used to seeing but always on God's timing—not mine. Having read *The Minister's Life of Obedience*, Mia and I learned more about how to be obedient to God's purpose for our lives, so we pressed into the Bible with renewed excitement and anticipation for what would come next in our relationship with each other and in our walk with Christ. Regardless of my career situation, Mia and I had become close again, so much so that we were discussing the possibility of marriage, though we agreed to wait on the Lord's timing.

Christmas is near and dear to Mia, a time when she combines the celebration of Christ's birth with giving to those less fortunate and focusing on family. She shares the importance of these things with her sons who were teenagers at this time. Being a homeless guy, I was a perfect candidate for Mia's attention and generosity she normally extends to the downtrodden, so she decided it was time to let me get a little closer to her boys. She had me over to help with the tree trimming, during which we were rewarded with hot chocolate and a nice dinner.

I was close with my parents, so recent December holidays had not been happy since dad passed on Christmas night six years prior, and then mom followed a while after. It still brings tears to recall how my appreciation of the season was restored by my love of Christ and Mia's loving gesture that turned into a beautiful evening. In fact, that evening my father's favorite song came on: Bing Crosby's "I'm Dreaming of a White Christmas." Naturally this weepy-hearted Christian again let loose with the waterworks, which was a bit embarrassing, but Mia and her boys showed me grace for the uncontrollable emotion. Also having a close relationship with both her parents, Mia somewhat understood how tough their absence must be at holidays. Her comforting during my time of weakness was something special. I will always cherish that wonderful—and clean and sober—Christmas experience of 2013.

Besides all that joy, I got to celebrate the year I found a perfect, loving relationship with my Heavenly Father. That holiday season could not have gone better—or so I thought. What about Mia's present? I needed a miracle. As God often does in the lives of Christians (certainly with Mia and me), He opened a door at the eleventh hour. On the Monday after that beautiful dinner with Mia and her boys, I was back to popping price tags onto clothing when the warehouse manager walked over to my station. He was an authoritative, authentically southern gentleman who had a daily mountain of donated items to deal with, leaving little time for small talk, so he got right to point:

"Hey boy, can you drive a truck?"

I immediately replied:

"Yes, sir! You bet I can!"

The position paid $14 per hour, and I was grateful to him and God for the opportunity. As a bonus, this was a cool job to get because of the connection with my father, who was a truck driver in the Teamsters Union; he had more than twenty-five years of on-the-road experience. But as the enemy often does, he smacked me in the face with past transgressions that were set to destroy this bit of hope for the future. But throughout the challenges to follow, the Holy Spirit had me keep faith by relying on the words of Paul in Romans 8:31:

> *"If God is for us, who can be against us?"*

Even when a person becomes radically transformed by God, it turns out the world still remembers traffic tickets and a suspended driver's license—major problems for someone wanting to drive professionally. This job offer had been my first hope of employment in many months, but the road to it was blocked. Again, I challenged God about why He was allowing so much opposition against His servant who had been diligently answering His call to righteousness. Was this the devil trying to thwart God's plan, or the Lord revealing areas of my life that needed pruning?

Either way, this was a time I needed to use God's Word against any carnal thoughts of potentially twisting the truth to get the job. In John 15, Jesus clearly lets us know He is the vine and Christians are His branches, so we can do nothing apart from Him. We need to do what He would do, and as professing Christians we must consider how our activity reflects on Him. To obey Christ, I had to take captive this interaction with the warehouse manager by coming clean with him; we stop the enemy through transparency. Regardless of how difficult it might be to always tell the truth, in John 8:32 Jesus lets us know the liberating reward for our honesty:

> *"You will know the **truth** [another name for **Jesus**] and the truth shall set you free."*

The old me would have wallowed in self-pity and made excuses for my messed-up driving record. But Jesus is the Way, the Truth, and the Life, so when we believe and follow Him, we are disciples of the truth, set free to be honest in all things. To have any shot at becoming a Salvation Army truck driver, this moment would be about facing the wreckage of my past and its resulting consequences. I immediately let the warehouse manager know my huge issue and exactly how it came about from the irresponsible depravity in my past. Apparently, that willingness to admit my mistakes caused the hardened boss to give this Christianized price-tagger some hope:

> *"Well boy, it looks like you'll need to get that mess cleaned up so we can put you in the driver's seat of one of them there trucks."*

This was God's grace at work! In a world without our Savior's influence, there is no way he would have allowed me to get behind the wheel of any Salvation Army vehicle, let alone a huge truck that displays their mission statement:

"Doing the most good!"

Now came the hard part: after several calls to the Pinellas Country DMV, I learned that $1200 was required to handle the fines and restore my license. I mentioned the cost to my warehouse manager, and he knew my present situation would not supply that kind of money. His hands were tied, but he promised me the job *if* I could somehow clean up my mess. He added:

"Until then, I will not be able to put your butt in the driver's seat of any truck."

By now you know my fitting routine of submitting to the Lord by hitting my knees. I questioned God about this seemly insurmountable issue for a guy making little more than $100 per month. I quickly dismissed the idea of asking Mia for the money, something that would surely put another strain on our relationship—I would not risk it. But then the Holy Spirit brought to mind my Christian brother Blake, the friend who gave me back my life by getting me into the ARC program. I felt the Holy Spirit declare:

"My servant Blake was there when you needed to find Me. He will help you again now."

Though this directive was from the Lord, and I had been greatly humbled by the fall from a six-digit income to being homeless, pride was still strong in my life, especially now that I was clean and sober. I thought more highly of myself than I ought, believing I needed no one's help. As shown in my overreaction to being denied the Hillsong concert, pride was a core issue keeping me from better walking in God's will, a stumbling block that keeps the vast majority of men and women from experiencing all God has for them. A lifetime of unrighteousness does not go away easily, so this became another opportunity for God to continue purging me of worldliness.

After all he had already done, it was tough calling Blake for another huge favor. I began by expressing my gratefulness for his help, but then resisted asking him for anything else; that is, until the humility found in Christ's strength rose up and I began to tell him about my awful financial hurdle. He asked for my plan to address the problem, and when it was only prayer at that point, God answered my plea through Blake—again. My Christian brother said:

"Well, I guess we better get over there and take care of this so you can start working and pay me back as soon as possible."

I agreed and endlessly thanked him for his continued willingness to step up, but with the DMV only open during business hours, I could not go because of the clothes-tagging work that paid my room and board. I also had to fill out a job application and get a doctor's physical. But the Lord also cast these problems aside. Through the grace of God's perfect timing, the warehouse manager wanted me driving before Christmas, so he ended my pricing career and had me immediately go handle whatever I must. After many long months jobless, at the eleventh-hour God had dished out the entire solution in just a few minutes. It again reminded me of Romans 8:31, a passage I had not full-heartedly accepted until this miraculous intervention—just one more of many—by my Heavenly Father:

> *"If God is for us, who can be against us?"*

Clearly, the Lord was in the truck-driver's seat. Within two days I had the application and physical completed, and Blake was picking me up in the afternoon to go salvage my standing with the Pinellas County DMV. This was all getting done quickly to meet the warehouse manager's need to have me working by the next day. So here I was sitting at the DMV contemplating another of God's fixes coming at the eleventh hour, and how that has been my favorite number since the Lord stamped it on my baseball uniform as young boy. What happened next was another amazing God-incident: I understand I am reaching with this one and I'm certainly not endorsing numerology with its "lucky" numbers, but consider that we were sitting there in front of twenty-five DMV windows and agents when I turned to my biblically solid friend Blake and boldly announced:

"Well brother, things certainly seem to be lining up; it would not surprise me if all this mess gets put behind me when we're called up to window eleven."

Blake snickered in disbelief but gave a confident comment on God's abilities:

"Sure, why not?"

As you've no doubt guessed, five minutes later it felt like God winking at us when we were called to window eleven. In a few short minutes my fines were paid, and we went back to waiting, this time for the window where my license would be reinstated. We sat joking about what had happened with the number, and then I asked Blake what he thought were the chances of us getting window eleven again. Of course, God knew I would forever glorify His name by telling this story to anyone who will listen—like you right now—so we got window eleven for a second time; I enjoyed the look on Blake's face as he witnessed God's power.

Right after the DMV, Blake unexpectedly asked me to call my last insurance company and see what it would cost to reinstate insurance on my car parked in his garage. He jokingly blamed himself by feigning the hardship of my vehicle taking up too much space. With another lightning bolt from God in the eleventh hour, my vehicle insurance was reactivated, *freeing* me to drive my old car again.

As we headed back to Tampa from Pinellas County (Clearwater and Saint Petersburg), I was once again close to tears from so much gratitude in my heart. I knew it was all God's doing through His disciple Blake. My old workplace was along the way, so we stopped in to see my previous boss, Bill. I wanted to show him what God had done. Bill was happy for me, and it was a joyful visit.

When we got to Blake's house, he handed over my car keys—with an additional $200 for a couple tanks of gas and a Christmas gift for Mia. Driving away I could not help weeping, while profusely thanking the Lord for His unmerited favor. The next morning would be my first day driving for the Salvation Army. Before leaving for work, I saw an email from Mia where she was passing along a post from a ministry headed by Ryan LeStrange, one of God's modern-day prophets. Here's what the message said:

> *"It just takes one moment to launch onto another level. . . In a single moment David was plucked out of the field and placed in the palace. . . Some of you have been hidden in a place of preparation but there will come a divine moment that will launch you forth. . . Don't be weary or defeated. . . God has not forgotten what he has declared over your life. . . He is molding you and shaping you. . . Destiny takes time. . . If you are obedient. . . You will be ready when the moment comes. . . Then spring forth and seize your moment!"*

Now, there was an appropriately timed message about obediently waiting on God's timing!

16

"Christmas Bonus— And Then Some!"

On Christmas Eve I ran out to get Mia a couple presents, and I was so grateful to drive again after nine months without wheels—try having no vehicle for a while. From my smile that lasted at least two days, you would have thought my worn-out, 12-year-old Chevy Cavalier was a new Mercedes convertible. In fact, when some church friends first saw me drive up, they chuckled and called it my "hooptie." But I didn't care because I had wheels again and they felt like wings.

For me, that unoffended attitude was a welcome sign that I was beginning to understand humility, something I *still* struggle with today. Like so many other Christians, when I have neglected time for God's Word each day, life's worldly deceptions cause pride to creep back in and hypocrisy follows. There is nothing more destructive to the Christian image than a prideful believer, an off-putting believer the world will reject, along with Jesus.

Strapped into my Chevy hooptie and under strict orders from Mia to not go overboard on spending for her, I set out to get her a few inconsequential presents that would be simple, but hopefully meaningful. Mia invited me to Christmas dinner and a gift exchange with her mother and incredible boys, and there she showered me with much needed new clothes. Although grateful that the Salvation Army had given me some thrift-store garb, Mia was tired of seeing me in nothing but hand-me-downs. It was close to my 11pm curfew when we finished exchanging presents, so I got up and started heading for the door—to drive *myself* home!—when Mia surprised me with one last present: she announced a trip to St. Augustine on Florida's upper Atlantic coast, a town established in 1565 by Spanish explorers and the oldest continuously inhabited settlement in the United

States. A few times Mia had mentioned how I needed to experience the special town with her someday. And through God's goodness, my work schedule had me with two days off at just the right time.

Mia has loved St. Augustine and had wonderful memories of it since family vacations there as a young girl. Later, her mother and brother moved to the historic town. For Christmas Mia gave me a much smaller version of the town's enormous, beautiful landmark cross that has a special place in her heart because of the many answered prayers she made from the foot of it.

In forty-four years of living in Florida, I had never been to St. Augustine, so this vacation at the end of 2013 was the cherry on top of a fulfilling year—kicked off by a new relationship with my Savior. I also found "the one," made it nine months clean and sober, and got an honorable job where I was helping the Salvation Army with "Doing the Most Good." This St. Augustine vacation would be a Christmas bonus, and then some.

Several weeks prior to this trip, Blake had a New Year's party planned, and one of the highlights was a baptismal ceremony for anyone wanting to bring in 2014 God's way. Mia was baptized as a small child and had been baptized a couple years prior when she rededicated her life and I as a small child, but since I had not knowingly confessed my faith at that time, we decided to both be baptized again—together as a symbol of our past relationships washed away.

We also vowed to continue honoring the Lord by remaining intimately pure until marriage, and the date for that was looking like it might be June 8th, 2014's Day of Pentecost. That date seemed to keep coming up, but it was only six months away, I still lived at the Salvation Army, and my job did not pay enough to settle my debt with Blake yet, let alone pay for a wedding and then support a family of four. Of course, that was the *natural*, worldly situation where circumstances appear impossible, but as our story demonstrates over and over, we serve a *supernatural* God.

The day we left for my first trip to St. Augustine, Mia and I got a late start because my shift did not end until 7pm. Then after showering, shaving, and driving to Mia's, we didn't finish the four-hour drive until well after our planned arrival at midnight. We spent a short time at her mother's house before going on to find someplace to stay. Unfortunately, neither of us had considered that Christmas in St. Augustine is a huge tourist draw with their traditional *Night of Lights,* when the town is decorated with millions of tiny white lights.

We ended up driving back and forth around the St. Augustine Beach area. After quite a while— and with little hope left—Mia recalled seeing a vacancy sign at a *motel* close to the Bridge of Lions. Being desperate at that point, we pulled in anyway and rang the bell at a window. Several minutes passed before a nice Indian man let us know they only had one room left on the second floor, and it would be $77 to stay in room 222 that night. Hearing the cost got me thinking this encounter might be God ordained: Mia's favorite number is 7. As God's number of completion and perfection, it's the most prominent digit in the Bible, including how 7 is emphasized in Genesis. In 6 days, God made the heavens, earth, and everything in them, after which He rested on the 7th day, calling His entire creation good (the enemy would later try to corrupt it, but that's another story).

I told the kind man we would take it, but upon reaching our room, the accommodations were not what either of us was accustomed to—and yes, that is saying a lot from a homeless guy bunking at the Salvation Army. Being the wee hours of the morning, we decided to stick it out, get some much-needed rest, and look for another place the next day. That night seemed to be another of God's lessons in humility, overcoming pride, and in a few hours when we awoke, Mia looked around and decided:

There is a reason God put us in this room, and as much as I do not want to stay here, I believe we need to. God chose a stable as the birthplace for His own Son, so who are we to want to turn down the literal last room at the last inn.

Having the same feeling that we were meant to be there, I agreed. But this was a cold, gray, rainy, miserable day, which meant we would not be able to see the gigantic cross Mia loved, so we spent most of the day visiting her nephew, her brother, and her brother's wife. Mia also took me to historic downtown St. Augustine, and even with the rain coming down on those old narrow streets—some maybe just a bit wider than a horse and buggy—we managed to visit a few shops. Later that evening after dinner with family, the deluge finally ended, so we took a trolley tour of the wondrous Christmas lights and then headed back to our little motel for some much-needed rest.

Our plan the next day was a trek to Mia's favorite cross that she was adamant about showing me.

The foot of it would be the perfect spot for praying together. From the beginning, our relationship had been God-breathed, so there was no more-appropriate spiritual place for her to share with her best friend and future husband. Even the world understands that life can be better when experienced together through marriage, but the enemy often deceives us into thinking that we do not need a help mate and that remaining single is the most desirable path. Even some Christians use this quote from Apostle Paul out of context:

"Now to the unmarried and the widows I say: It is good for them to stay unmarried, as I do."

The full passage is Paul telling those who have received the gift of marriage to stay with it, but others like him should remain single *if* that is God's calling on their lives. God's grand design was not for Adam to be alone while trimming trees, pruning plants, naming rodents, and riding zebras (praise God there were initially no thorns and there will not be any in the new heavens and earth to come). Like the Lord, men and women made in His image also thrive on companionship, and a godly marriage can produce one of the most productive and joyful relationships, secondary only to a personal relationship with the actual Creator of the entire universe.

But again, if you are like Paul, go ahead and stay single so you can fully focus on what God would have you do for His kingdom. On the other hand, if marriage is in your future—as it is for much of mankind—it is an incredible covenant God uses to teach us selflessness, respect, love, patience, understanding, giving, listening, and much more. Putting the needs of another before your own is what our world needs, as opposed to these recent *me-generations* that the world has been selling us, an inward focus leading to a shallow, unsatisfying life. Instead, our lives will gravitate toward love, peace, and joy if only we would follow God's edict to put Him and others above ourselves.

We awoke early on an extremely cold day, and because our modest room had no way to make coffee, I went out to find some. Once back on that crystal clear day with a bright blue sky, Mia suggested we open the curtains to let the sun in and crack a window open for fresh, crisp air. Room 222 was on the end of the second floor, so it was the only one with a side window. Mia drew back the curtains before struggling with a ridiculously stuck window, which meant I had the chance to play hero, so I came over and we opened it *together*. With some welcome sun and a cool breeze coming in, we grabbed our coffees and sat down on the bed to enjoy the view. In the next moment, our astonished faces turned back to each other; off in the distance and directly centered in our window was the St. Augustine cross! Once again God was showing off in a way that we would easily recognize as having happened through Him.

Later we were able to reach that cross, and Mia was right about how wonderful it was being in the presence of that majestic, *huge* cross (Pic on the next page), especially since I was with my best friend for life. The experience was beyond words. We felt the Holy Spirit's presence as we joined hands and knelt together below the cross, lifting our hearts to God, putting our relationship in the Lord's hands, and asking for direction on how we were to proceed *together*.

While we drove back to Tampa that afternoon through the beautiful Ocala National Forest, Mia phoned her mother. She mentioned how room 222 was special because it was the last available place to stay in St. Augustine during those wee hours and our window had the motel's only view of the cross. Then her mom added more. Something we wouldn't know. She said:

"Well, Mia, you were born in a room 222."

It was just more confirmation and not so surprising because those sorts of incidents were becoming a pattern that reflects the miracle-working power involved when the Lord communicates with us.

We got back to Tampa in time for me to say goodbye to Mia, hop into the hooptie, and make Sally by curfew. What an amazing time with her, and the St. Augustine cross will forever be etched on my heart—later, you will see why it took on even more meaning.

New Year's Eve was a bit about discussing wedding plans, but mostly for bringing in 2014 with our Bible study family. We prepared our hearts before being baptized at midnight.

Although we were baptized separately that night, after each of us went below the water and came up, we were ready to live life together for God. Mia and I received much prayer on that special evening, and when we reflected on 2013, we felt blessed to have such an incredibly spiritual church family supporting us, especially during those times when a future together was looking less likely. The year that was all about taking God's hand and then Him putting Mia's hand in mine ended with God, Mia, and me hand-in-hand during December—a Christmas bonus and then some!

17

"New Year, New Direction"

With 2013 behind us, Mia and I took seriously our New Year's Eve declaration of devotion to God, where we pledged to continue walking by faith instead of worldly sight. We vowed to follow the Holy Spirit's direction, crucifying our flesh whenever necessary (frequently). We wanted to be married and neither of us was interested in the traditions of dating several months, followed by a lengthy engagement. However, the date God put on our hearts, June 8th, was just five months away. The issue with a huge delay was not so much about an irresistible, physical attraction—though that was there!—but more because it meant quickly pulling off a large wedding with me as a low-income driver and Mia as a stay-at-home mom.

We were up for the challenge but, once again, God would have to perform a miracle *if* we were to be married in June. There would be much planning necessary to properly honor this union our Savior put together. I don't mean to denigrate a rapid and thrifty marriage: even the Apostle Paul in 1 Corinthians 7:9 sounded okay with just getting it done:

> *"If they cannot control themselves, they should marry, for it is better to marry than to burn with passion."*

But because Mia and I were so grateful for all the Lord was doing (to make us *better together*), we wanted an event which would greatly glorify God—in His eyes, the church's eyes, and the eyes of the world. The goal was a significant production that would include our church family and Mia's boys, allowing them to fully witness what God had orchestrated so they could praise him and also glorify the Lord by telling the story.

All that said, *if* God was going to help us put everything together in only five months, we needed assistance above the merged financial means of a home mom and Salvation Army driver. We continued maintaining our prayer life, walking closely with Christ, and being obedient to His Word, a combination that propels Christians toward stronger faith. We were all about following the Spirit's lead in the supernatural realm, while lessening our trust in the natural world we could see.

While Mia continued being a phenomenal mother, helping others, and attending classes at Life Christian University, I worked extensive hours as a driver who also unloaded the trucks, sometimes by myself depending on whether I arrived before the store employees. Those nontypical solo mornings of heavy labor made it hard to crucify my flesh and not be prideful from being a college graduate who formerly had a six-figure income and was now in a position below my former social status, making only $14 per hour to help the Salvation Army do "the most good." Five or six hours of lifting heavy furniture for $75 was a far cry from my previous high paying, cushy desk job. Still, I was grateful to be employed, and again, Sally also covered my room and board.

I knew God created me for more than that position, but I settled into waiting on God's timing, knowing my job was part of His plan. I imagine He was teaching me to persevere at a humble attitude and self-control (no matter what my work), two things I have personally struggled with throughout my life. So, I kept driving and unloading with a smile on my face and a spring in my step. Between stops I would have heart-to-heart talks with God about whether this was where He wanted me. I was not ungrateful or angry about where He had me; my concern was only for becoming a better provider if *He* was going to have Mia and me marry June 8th.

While conversing with my Savior one day in mid-January, I sensed that He was ready to open a new door, and I increasingly knew that I knew He was orchestrating another beginning. In fact, the feeling got so strong, I called Mia and could barely contain myself when telling her God had something big coming. I asked her to pray in agreement that our Heavenly Father was getting ready to bless me financially to help us pull off the wedding. Mia agreed, so I knew His promise would come to pass, as they always do after Christians make a request that is in alignment with His Word and will for their lives.

The next day while I was driving, my phone rang, and I recognized the number as my dear friend Bill. After our visit to the DMV, he was my previous boss who Blake and I had stopped by to see, say hello, and mention the miracles God was working in my life. Apparently, that day had an impact on him, and he could not explain what it was, but he said there had been something different about me; he knew my life had been forever changed. Bill asked if I was still driving for the Salvation Army and then made this offer:

> *"Well, knowing you have really turned the corner and I've seen the remarkable change in you myself, I was wondering if you would consider coming back to work for me?"*

Bill had always paid handsomely, so I was floored and wanted to immediately take the job, but in obedience to the Lord, I thanked him for the incredibly generous opportunity and let him know I needed to pray for God's guidance. Bill told me to take my time. The job was mine. Wow!

Some may say this was just another coincidence, but the predictability and regularity of these divine happenings make them easily recognizable as God-incidents. We Christians must stop doubting and denying our Heavenly Father's ability to openly reward His children for their faith and obedience to His Word. If you haven't already, I pray you too find this for your life. An intimate journey with God means walking in His promises— and He *never* fails to make good on them. It may not happen for you as immediately as it did for me, but when you stay in His will, His promises *will* come to pass. So, live your life by it. Believe it. Claim it. Though doing so is not always easy, we must follow the old saying: let go and let God. It's the *"only* way to soar," as God tells us in Isaiah 40:31, and with Proverbs 3:5–6 He promises to keep us on the right track:

> *"But those who hope in the LORD will renew their strength. They will soar on wings like eagles; they will run and not grow weary, they will walk and not be faint."*

> *"Trust in the Lord with all you heart and lean not on your own understanding. In all your ways submit to Him, and He shall make your paths straight"*

Be more than a conqueror, never forgetting that we can count on *every* promise our Lord made through the Bible (there are a lot of them) and those He tells us personally. You will know when the latter happens.

God had supernaturally answered our prayer for marriage provision, and I immediately shared the amazing news with Mia before asking her to pray with me about how to proceed. Yes, taking Bill's offer seemed like a no-brainer, but the Salvation Army helped me recover from addiction, provided a bed and food—put me in the room where I met Christ!—provided the months of security this baby Christian needed while Jesus forever transformed my life, and even gave me an opportunity to get through Christmas with some dignity.

So, the decision was not as easy as it seemed, but by seeking the Holy Spirit's direction, having Mia intercede through prayer, and consulting with our church family, I took the job. Unlike my previous days of my decisions being driven by worldly flesh and financial considerations, a major reason I chose the job was to be on that fertile witnessing ground of my old job where there were few Christ followers. Rather than continue in my cocoon at the Salvation Army, surrounded by like-minded believers who could demonstrate a godly life, this new, old place was now where I could do the most good. God had me go where I could be of maximum service as one of His lights shining in the darkness.

Of course, working at this secular company would also test and strengthen my faith: I would need godly perseverance with the guys who only knew me as an enthusiast partier. As Daniel was supernaturally protected by God, I would need to rely on Him during my time in this lion's den but having grown confident in Christ's blood as my protection, I felt Daniel's anointing on my life and was excited to throw myself into that cage. The next day I called Bill and jumped back into the fishing industry; this time it would be as much about making a sufficient living as fishing for men.

But first I needed to give two weeks' notice and wanted to offer my appreciation to the tough warehouse manager at the Salvation Army. I walked up, let him know about the new job, and profusely thanked him for the opportunity to represent the Salvation Army after they had saved my life, given me the roadmap for a relationship with Christ, and put me back into society—singing a song of hope. I had not expected his response: he was completely unhappy that I would take another opportunity, told me not to bother with the two weeks, and said I had worked my last day there, so I needed to pack my things and find somewhere else to live.

I could not believe my ears and even chuckled a bit while calling him out for joking. But there was no hint of a smile on his hardened face; instead, he suggested I should have given the decision more thought, mentioned how hard he had pulled for me, and talked about how his efforts had been for my protection. Perplexed about that last one, I asked what he meant, after which he explained that most people coming out of rehab need a solid year before getting back into the world's corrupting system. He was genuinely concerned about keeping me sober. It was a valid point. Was he right? Would I fail? I could relapse from taking this great-paying job, working for a company with worldly principles—rather than continuing to do the most good for God's army. He leaned in and leveled a serious challenge:

"Will you change your mind now and stick it out for a year before making a decision to reenter the real world?"

At that point I knew he genuinely cared and was trying to do me a favor. But unlike many others he had dealt with, I was completely sold out for Jesus, burning with a desire to serve Christ's kingdom. I get it, he had seen too much rehab failure over the years to trust that my faith had provided full recovery. This interaction with him reminded me of a few weeks earlier when he found out about my relationship to Mia. He got in my face to warn that I would fall. No wonder he was fired up from concern: here I was giving notice, confirming his previous warning.

I know he had sound reasoning from all the rehab failures he had witnessed, but this time God was going to have him see real faith in action, a way to provide him with more hope. God wanted him to learn that drug addicts who are radically transformed by the King of kings are certainly not destined to repeat the worldly ways of their old selves. For now, he would go on looking for me to reenter the program—or die. But I had already died to myself and was living out a demonstration of Christ. I was confident that the Lord would someday and somehow update him on my godly progress. Sadly, Floyd relapsed and died. All of us are potentially *one* bad decision away from what could be the end. It breaks my heart that he bypassed his own advice. His passing is a humble reminder of how much I need Jesus every waking moment of my life.

After my extremely difficult resignation from the Salvation Army, my new future would begin with an immediate need for housing. I faced an urgent and difficult situation where the Lord had not yet intervened to show me the path forward. Was it the 11th hour yet again? Yes, it was. I simply lifted my heart and asked, "Father, what do I do?" These sorts of issues used to make me panic, but by this time I had learned to keep faith in Jesus, stand on God's Word, and wait—even if by the minute— on the Holy Spirit's direction. While packing to move out, I continued praying deeply for answers and then called Bill to see if I could start the following Monday. Answering another prayer, he said, "absolutely!" Now I needed a temporary home and living with Mia was *not* an option. After more appealing to the Spirit, I felt Him give what was becoming a familiar response:

"Have you considered my servant Blake?"

Of course, it would be him, again: my Christian brother had stood by me from the beginning, all through God's monumental transformation of my life. Though I still owed Blake a thousand dollars, I had been paying him back weekly, and after I mentioned the new high-paying job and how the warehouse manager kicked me out, Blake was 100% in my corner—though astonished by the harsh move-out order. I explained that the manager wanted me to stay for honorable reasons. Because the housing situation was run by a different division, even though Blake was on the Salvation Army board, he could not help with the decision to have me suddenly vacate my room at the Sally. But knowing how my heart had been transformed by Christ, he did not share the manager's concerns and could see why I would want to step out on faith, especially with marriage only five months away.

In another demonstration of Blake's godly generosity, he offered me a room in his house—rent free. But he also kept me accountable for my obligations by having me promise to continue repaying the loans, even while saving for my own place and a wedding (Lord willing). How's that for 2014's new direction?! God is good!

18

"Course Change Comes with a Price"

While grabbing my belongings at the Salvation Army and heading to Blake's house, I had a peace inside from knowing this decision was Spirit led. Though I would not yet have my own place, and marriage to Mia was still a while down the road, my friend's continued kindness meant my own bedroom and bathroom—for the first time in nine months. I had been sharing my room with five guys and a community bathroom with one hundred fifty. Driving to Blake's I sensed God's presence, followed by this Romans 8 passage coming to mind:

> *"And we know that in all things, God works for the good of those who love Him, who have been called according to His purpose. For those God foreknew He also predestined to be conformed to the image of His Son, that He might be the firstborn among many brothers and sisters. And those He predestined, He also called; those He called, He also justified; those He justified, He also glorified."*

God's Word never fails, and when we walk with Him, He loves to overwhelm us with generosity (like Blake's beautiful swimming pool and his very large house on the Hillsborough River). When we wait on God and trust Him to intervene, He often does so in conspicuous ways that clearly show Who's responsible for such unmerited favor. That way we understand it was the Lord's doing and give Him the glory; in that way we point others toward God.

Extremely grateful to God and Blake, I moved into my new digs, but they came at a price—a test. First though, Blake handed over a key, gave me the lay of the land, and trusted me with the alarm code. Because he often traveled out of town for business, he asked that I set the alarm when away during the day, and suggested I keep it activated at night while sleeping. Though I suddenly had privacy, this new freedom would take some getting used to.

The Salvation Army had many rules (understandable for a home full of addicts), and we were surrounded by accountability partners who checked our sobriety every time we re-entered the facility, including urine and breathalyzer tests. But now I had a plush home, and the owner was often away, leaving me free to do as I pleased without fear of being caught—the perfect setup for the first real challenge I would face as a recovering addict. Before explaining what happened, I want to acknowledge how God's goodness can come to us in dreams: a week before moving in with Blake, I dreamed about being at a party holding a glass of wine and sneaking a peek in a kitchen cupboard where I found a bottle of prescription Percocet—my addiction drug. The sight of those little pills immediately fired up the endorphins, setting my brain ablaze and solidifying an uncontrollable need to take them. In this dream, I quickly threw four or five in my mouth, chased them down with a gulp of wine, and immediately felt deep guilt and self-condemnation flow into my soul.

The dream had been so vivid it took me a minute after I woke up to understand it was not real. I shared the nightmare with Mia and then mostly forgot it over the next week—until a couple nights after moving into Blake's house. He was out of town, and I was not feeling well, so I decided to turn in early. About 3am I awoke with one of the worst headaches I've ever experienced, a wicked—maybe literally—shooting pain.

Not knowing what headache medicine Blake might have, I began searching kitchen cabinets for ibuprofen. Finding only vitamins, I dug deeper, grabbing and examining each label—until I found myself holding a bottle of Percocet! They were left over from Blake's shoulder surgery a year earlier. He had only taken a couple since he worked so closely with addicts and well knew the potential addiction issues (like mine). So, there they sat in my hand, igniting my brain. With a throbbing headache now exponentially worse from firing endorphins, I immediately felt sick to my stomach and recognized just how real and evil the devil is.

As quickly as I thought how despicable Lucifer is for tempting me like that, I remembered the previous week's dream, now understanding that it was vivid because my wonderful Heavenly Father had given me a useful vision. Instantly all those feeling of guilt and condemnation from taking the dream pills flooded my confused brain, giving me a revulsion for my formerly favorite pharmaceutical. I put them back in place and eventually found some ibuprofen.

With that monumental victory, God erased any desire I might have had to revisit that bottle before Blake returned. When he did get back, I went to the cupboard, pulled out the Percocet, and handed it to him. At first, he was angry and wanted to know how I even found them, but after I explained he confirmed none were missing and was grateful that I had quickly told him the truth. This became an excellent opportunity for Blake to see how much my relationship with Christ meant to me: *nothing* was going to come between my walk with Christ and His plans for Mia and me.

I quickly got into a routine of rising early and commuting thirty miles to work. The income was high enough that I was able to pay Blake back quickly and become the gentleman who could take my Mia on dates. It felt amazing. After five months of waiting to experience some sort of normalcy in our relationship, I was elated at another sudden and radical change God made in my life: I could call Mia, ask her out, drive myself to her house, bring flowers, and actually pay for dinner. How cool is that!? My appreciation of the ability continues today as I do my best to keep dating Mia.

She and I were becoming closer and closer, even with my long workdays and an hour commute that was perfect for listening to Scripture without distraction, such as the Bible readings done by Max McLean on the Bible Gateway app. As Romans 10:17 tells us:

> *"So then faith cometh by hearing, and hearing by the word of God."*

Mia and I continued Thursday night Bible studies with our church family at TCF and Saturday evening services at Grace Family Church. She was approaching the end of her first year attending classes at Life Christian University, and we discussed me possibly joining her in the fall. So, we were experiencing many of God's blessings and all was progressing well—until one day in February when life slapped me across the face. Fortunately, though, this was ten months into walking with Jesus, meaning I had been putting on the armor of God for a while and was equipped with Scripture like Isaiah 54:17:

> *"No weapon formed against you shall prosper."*

No matter how much Bible study makes us harder to corrupt, the devil still attempts to frustrate, disarm, and otherwise challenge every Christian. Those living in the Tampa Bay area are familiar with Satan's use of the Howard Franklin Bridge to bring out the worse in humanity. The seven-mile span between Tampa and St. Petersburg has many lanes that often slow to a crawl with heavy traffic, so much so that signs are posted on each end, telling travelers to check gas levels before getting on.

That morning I was only a third of the way across when my attention went to the dashboard where a tiny light had come on and the temperature gauge was spiking, meaning my old car was overheating. For over five miles I fervently pleaded with the Lord to help me last until I was off the bridge. He divinely answered when the engine of my smoking and chugging hooptie seized up, but not until I was pulling into the first gas station. I had it towed to a mechanic's garage, but with a blown engine it was no longer worth much, so the mechanic offered me $400 and sold my junker to a junkyard for parts. Even him giving me that much demonstrated God's unmerited favor because the car wasn't worth more than $500 when it was running.

My gracious Lord wasn't done: that evening He sent even more help, and of course it was through His servant—my housemate and official guardian angel in human form—who provided a transportation solution: Blake heard my situation and called Jay, a mutual friend in the wholesale car business who "happened" to have a mint-condition 1998 Mercedes-Benz C280. Jay felt that car would work well in my financial situation, but since I had only recently gotten a better job and I'd been paying Blake back, I only had a thousand dollars saved, plus the $400 coming from the mechanic who junked my hooptie. With more divine favor through Jay's willingness to help, I got an amazing deal at only $2300 out the door. Before I could even ask, Blake volunteered the extra thousand and jokingly added:

"Don't worry, you're good for it. Besides, I know where you live."

I was able to purchase the Mercedes outright, transfer my hooptie tags to it, and be back at work by noon the next day. Though it was in my name, Blake rightly held the title as collateral until I paid him back. Reflecting back, I am amazed to think how the old Robby would have gone through all kinds of turmoil with that sort of situation, but this time while walking with God there was no discouragement; peace came over me and my faith never wavered, knowing He would help me through. Again Romans 10:18 comes to mind:

> *"We know that in all things God works for the good of those who love Him, who have been called according to His purpose."*

Part of the price I paid to continue living in God's promises was to reject that Percocet—just not pop them in my mouth. Christians will continually pay personalized prices to remain obedient to God and His Word, but those requirements will always be insignificant compared to what He did for every one of us on the cross.

19

"*Nothing* Is Impossible for Those Who Believe"

All was going well living at the beautiful home of my best-buddy Blake, who was playing the Apostle Paul in my life, walking beside me just as Paul did for young Timothy. Although bold at times, Blake's teaching style was less preaching and more about asking clarifying questions. Even writing this years later, I am overwhelmed with gratitude to my Christian brother and the Lord who made me his assignment. Every major crossroad I faced to that point involved Blake coming alongside to help keep my feet firmly planted in the Lord's Word and communing with Jesus—my Rock. Blake helped financially and spiritually. Like the Apostle Paul's dedication to Timothy, week by week while we were roommates, Blake continued pouring into my life.

Because Mia attended school one night each week and spent the remaining nights with her sons (except for weekends), Blake and I spent many evenings watching sermons from men of God like Joseph Prince, David Jeremiah, James McDonald, Ravi Zacharias, and John Hagee.

Although Mia's sons knew their mom was seeing me, I completely understood why she continued protecting them from any potential mental conflicts or future disappointment by not yet bringing me around much; I had faith that God would arrange those relationships in His time, not mine. My constant reliance in every situation became Bible passages like Mark 10:27: *"Jesus looked at them and said, 'With man this is impossible, but not with God; all things are possible with God.'"*

And like Mark's fellow disciple Paul, who was the ultimate defender of the faith, Blake's undeniable calling was Christian apologetics. We enjoyed talking about and tackling the tough questions coming from atheists, agnostics, and even professed believers struggling through doubt in some area of their walk with God. Blake is well seasoned in Scripture, so during those roommate days he gave me much of the study material I still use today.

That includes *The Baker Illustrated Bible Commentary* I left at Mia's house that she brought me before my trip to Lake Junaluska, a study Bible that has given me a much deeper understanding of God's Word. Accompanied by beautiful pictures throughout, this amazing resource breaks each Bible book down by who wrote it and when, as well as the audience for which it was intended. You may already know, but if not, I promise you won't regret grabbing a similar study Bible. While you *will* spiritually grow by just reading the Bible, you can gain a deeper understanding of where the Holy Spirit was coming from during the timeframe, He had each of the forty men write their part over those fifteen hundred years—Scripture will come to life like never before.

During that season before marriage, God had me live with Blake because He knew I needed quick growth in scriptural knowledge: He was calling me to spiritually lead a marriage where my future wife had been exposed to Christ since youth and was advancing to university studies in theology. The Lord yoked us together, so brother Blake's Bible mastery, along with his willingness to pour it into me each week, exponentially increased my understanding of Scripture in those pre-wedding months—praise God!

Blake was also supportive of my relationship with Mia and had been since he found out about her while he and I were roommates at the Lake Junaluska retreat. I revealed how God said she's the one, after which he had a front row seat for the Lord's miracles, signs, and wonders that followed. God creates mutual support systems for Christians, which was evident when He had Blake learn from witnessing the raging fires and blowing storms in my and Mia's relationship. Blake saw how God faithfully guided us to safety, while providing more spiritual growth. What he witnessed definitely affected his walk with the Lord, so our friendship has helped each of us in the way Solomon wrote about in Proverbs 27:17:

"As iron sharpens iron, so does one sharpen another."

While I was learning so much from Blake, God used Mia and me to show him that **nothing** *is impossible for those who believe.*

For what was happening by February 2014, a football analogy might be helpful, and I apologize in advance to those who may not appreciate the comparison. We'll call our two teams *true believers* (the underdogs) and *worldview* (heavy favorite). Mia and I will represent the former. The latter is vastly more popular, has overwhelming experience, and has a virtually unbroken streak of victories. In fact, *worldview* has shaped America significantly over the past hundred years, as evidenced by our formerly Christian-centered culture that has thrown God out of education, government, politics, sports, entertainment, and most all other public places—besides behind the closed doors of churches. Each new victory for *worldview* results in the further moral decline of society.

Of course, *true believers* promote godly character, so they understand and expect the mismatch because *worldview* offers what humans desire: cultural acceptance and doing whatever feels good as long as no one else gets hurt. *Worldview* promotes people fulfilling any and all fleshly desires, while everyone else must applaud or at least look the other way. Our formerly Christian society has instead become centered on a new sort of tolerance, something that used to mean loving the sinner but hating the sin. To be a "tolerant" person in our times, we are required to fully accept and even promote whatever adverse morals and behaviors anyone else has. If we do not support the deviance of others—with few exceptions—we are said to be intolerant. And unfortunately, even many Christians have bought into this lie. I'm sorry if my phrasing is more of a hammer than a nudge, but this concerns biblical truth. God's truth. *The* truth.

Though *true believers* have the odds stacked against them, Scripture details many examples of underdogs winning when it seemed impossible, like how the prophet Samuel was told by God to speak to Jesse about one of his eight sons becoming the king of Israel. Jesse brought out seven sons but passed over even considering David because of his youth and stature. Likewise, Mia and I on team *true believers*—half of which was a homeless, jobless, drug addict—stood virtually no chance of becoming husband and wife in just eleven months. From the moment God told me she was the one, that outcome seemed unreachable, especially within a year.

Like how my lowly situation appeared, 15-year-old David physically paled in comparison to King Saul, the first-ever king of Israel who was solidly built and at least a head taller than anyone else. But Saul was more concerned about himself than truly following God, often disappointing the Lord by ruling Israel with a *worldview* mentality. Based on size, King Saul would have been the Israelites' first choice to face Goliath, a nine-foot, six-inch giant. But looks can be deceiving. Though small, shepherd-boy David was his father Jesse's last resort for presenting to Samuel as a possible future king of Israel, but the Lord knew David was bold as a lion with his faith—he understood who he was in the Lord.

Mia's and my relationship culminating in a fairly quick marriage can be compared to the outward appearance of slightly built David taking on the massive Goliath. Like that future king of Israel, she and I were in agreement with God's game plan and knew *nothing is impossible for those who believe*. Early on, the Lord declared to both of us that we would be *better together*, but the defeat of *worldview* would take us sticking close to God and like-minded Christ followers. So, the *true believers* team was made up of more than Mia and me: we had godly brothers and sisters, our Heavenly Father as coach, Christ playing quarterback, and the Holy Spirit as offensive and defensive coordinator. Though our team looked like some pathetic addict and a mom going against the *worldview* titan, *true believers* had the Trinity, giving *worldview* no chance—the creation is no match for the Creator. In the natural world, underdog *true believers* appeared undersized, unequipped, and unpopular, but supernaturally we had an all-star Quarterback with a perfect pass-to-completion record and an undefeated Coach. Mia and I were the only weak links, so we just needed to follow Coach's game plan.

Of course, hopelessly human players have a hard time sticking to the plan. Like what a football player does when panicking during the action, Mia and I took it upon ourselves to change some plays on the fly, getting away from Coach's game plan because of what *worldview* was throwing at us. But our Coach is the Author of the future, so His game plan had already gotten victory for *true believers*—we just needed to not mess it up. Why would we ever second guess Jesus's quarterbacking when He obviously has everything under control, always? This interference by me and Mia only got us into fourth-and-long situations. I know there are times when a football player is expected to make changes during the play, and it can lead to positive yardage, but *true believers* need only follow what is laid out by the Coaches and Quarterback. And that means all Christian brothers and sisters who join *true believers* must also be compliant with the Trinity's leadership.

I laid all that out to get to this: if you have joined *true believers* with its divine guidance (Who never lose), why not *always* be obedient to execute God's will. When Mia and I stayed in alignment with God's game plan, what He laid out for us, our team was unstoppable. It only broke down when we didn't trust the Head Coach, listen to the Quarterback, or obey our Coordinator. But following the playbook—our Holy Bible—led to more and more points on the board and us realizing that *nothing* is impossible for *true believers*.

Hopefully this long—possibly painful—analogy will prompt some spectators to more fully commit to *team true believers Christian worldview*, resolving to become more valuable to the planetary fight by studying

God's game plan laid out in Scripture. The Lord's organization (*true believers*) faces a deadly battle with *team worldview's-worldview,* not just in and for this physical, earthly life, but also with eternity on the line. In the supernatural realm, *true believers* has a vast army of gargantuan, Christ-affirming warriors who are following God's game plan, so we have succeeded on more plays than not. Much fruit has already been seen for our efforts.

All that said, Mia and my local squad of *true believers* experienced some dicey action after Mia mentioned this:

"I know this may seem a bit selfish, but it is my heart's desire to have a black diamond for an engagement ring."

My prior experience with black diamonds was only on difficult snow-skiing runs, so my first thought was that it sounded expensive and hard to pull off in a few months; we had a long field to victory so why would we add more obstacles? I felt we needed to run with our heads down and punch this one into the end zone. But not wanting to let my teammate down, I tossed the ball back to her:

"Okay, what do you suggest we do?"

She suggested we first find out where we could get one, to which I replied that we should leave that for our Heavenly Coach. This meant I was immediately agreeing to Mia's dark gem; however, I also pointed out our financial situation—me still paying Blake back while also saving for the wedding. I asked whether she thought this expense was going to be more than we could handle. Mia rightly and calmly replied:

"God knows my heart. He will provide if it's meant to be."

Our Head Coach got to work, and it was apparent the next time Mia had her hair done. Like bartenders for the sober, hairstylists spark conversations with their robed captives, so the conversation eventually got around to the *true believers* story and the many miracles up to that point.

Keep in mind though, Mia understands how *worldview* makes up the majority of players on the field—most playing for the broad road instead of the narrow one (*true believers*)—so as Matthew 7:6 instructs, she is careful not to cast her pearls (biblical wisdom) in front of "swine," an indelicate word the Bible uses for those who reject any discussion of godly things. Christians must always witness to the lost, but like Matthew 10:14 says here, when it is apparent our thoughts are no longer welcome, we are to end it and move onto the next lost person:

> *"If anyone will not welcome you or listen to your words, leave that home or town and shake the dust off your feet."*

Even though Mia's hairstylist at that time was on team *true believers,* many of our Christian teammates remain doubters about God's miracles still happening in our time, an attitude *worldview* has successfully pushed on their uninformed Christian opponents. This causes *true believers* to doubt parts of their own faith, leading to botched plays or even some just sitting down on the field. They do not look for assistance through the signs, wonders, or miracles of our Great Intercessor and Quarterback Jesus, who always stands ready to help His bride (the church. . .every Christian).

This time there was no supernatural reference in Mia's comment about wanting a black diamond engagement ring, but from the next chair over, another stylist added a miracle for all the ladies to hear:

"Funny you mention that: my husband is serving in Afghanistan and recently purchased some black diamonds as an investment."

Mia had also had that stylist do her hair in the past. In fact, she even knew the woman's soldier husband, and it turned out he was set to return home in just a few weeks. Here was another huge gain on the field for *true believers*—and a military family's black diamond business. After her hair appointment, Mia immediately called me for a *true believers* celebration of what our divine Coach had *again* done. I was excited for Mia, but also a bit hesitant about the potential impact on our team's tight salary cap (low funds). But "hesitant" is just a less-incriminating way of saying "fearful," something that should be nowhere in the *true believers'* playbook, as the Lord tells us in 1 John 4:15–18:

> "God is love; whoever abides in love abides in God, and God in him. In this way, love has been perfected among us, so that we may have confidence on the day of judgment; for in this world we are just like Him. There is no fear in love, but perfect love drives out fear, because fear involves punishment. The one who fears has not been perfected in love."

Fear shows a lack of faith, which was not an issue for young David when he confidently faced a menacing giant that made all the hardened Israelite warriors cower. Unlike that future king, my black-diamond fears showed a lack of faith that would need to be overcome if *true believers* were going to win against *worldview.*

One day not long after Mia's divine encounter during her haircut, she showed me the social media profile of the hairstylist's husband and talked about her excitement to connect with him when he returned— whenever that might be. After this we went out to run errands and were talking more about him after brunch, then headed to grab dessert at a local establishment. Once inside and while waiting to order, something strange happened. A man came walking down the aisle toward us. With Mia's back turned toward him, I locked eyes with the guy, and he put a finger over his lips, seemingly signaling me to remain silent as he snuck up on Mia! My protection instincts kicked in, but he looked somewhat familiar and was a clean-cut young man, so I stayed on guard but let it happen. He reached Mia from behind and actually placed his hands over her eyes. Then in a strange voice he jokingly said:

"They really let you in here? Guess who?"

From his somewhat disguised voice, Mia could not tell who he was right away, so the man released her eyes, revealing him to be the same soldier we had just seen on social media that day. The fledgling black diamond dealer had made it home earlier than expected—adding to the story of this divine appointment. Mia introduced me and immediately wanted to view the diamonds. Of course, fearful, anxious me wasted little time before having to ask about cost. He laughed and replied:

"Don't sweat it; they're not as expensive as you think, and I've known Mia a long time so I will make sure she gets what she wants, and it won't break the bank."

I thanked him for his service to our country and for helping hurt *worldview* by fulfilling the heart's desire of my teammate on *true believers*. With my unfounded financial fears gone, this drive down the field had been one for the record books, and only happened from the goodness of our team leadership. In a city of over a million people, what is the mathematical probability that this young man we had just been discussing, a guy who recently got into the black diamond business and hadn't been home in over a year, would walk into the same building at the exact time we were there? The likelihood is virtually impossible; that is, without our Heavenly Coach's playbook, the Quarterback's lead, and obedience to the coordinator's instructions. When fully buying into the game plan on *team true believers,* the fatally flawed *worldview* squad has no chance—*all* things are possible for those who believe!

And for you who have graciously stuck with me through the entire football analogy, especially non-fans, I promise this book will attempt no more parallels to competitive sports.

20

"Our Wedding Plans?"

For me the most edifying Bible passages are those from Jesus, particularly His parables. Most of Scripture teaches us through real history, but the parables of Jesus have challenged me to search for the hidden manna among those beautifully spoken words from our King of kings. I love how He begins a parable with this sort of fantastical attention-grabber:

"The kingdom of heaven is like. . ."

We are drawn to learn about our future home and the place God lives. When writing this book, Mia and I asked the Holy Spirit to guide our words toward whatever would be most biblically helpful for readers and give God the greatest glory. Honoring that request, while deciding on this chapter's title, the Holy Spirit led me to a parable of Jesus that begins with Matthew 22:1–2:

"Jesus spoke to them again in parables saying: 'The kingdom of heaven is like a king who prepared a wedding banquet for his son.' "

Earlier I introduced that coincidences involving the number 222 have meaning in my and Mia's relationship, showing up as messages from the Lord. Again, we are not into numerology, but God uses many ways to grab people's attention, including numbers. And though I've read that passage many, many times since God revealed some significance surrounding Mia, me, and 222, the Lord waited until the day I would write the title of this chapter—"Our Wedding Plans?"—to use Matthew *22:2* as His way of telling us "our" wedding plans have actually been *His*. The verse is about God preparing a wedding for His Son, and because my and Mia's wedding plans were really His, that passage together with the chapter title confirmed what He declared to me on July 26th—that Mia is *the one*. This all made divine sense: Why wouldn't God prepare the wedding banquet for me? He is my King. I am His son.

By February we had the exact black diamond Mia's heart desired—praise God! She bought it on the spot, taking no chance of losing that beautiful, one-of-a-kind gem. The kind young soldier even supplied a jeweler friend who could mount the stone; he wanted to help her find someone trustworthy. I was thrilled and grateful to the Lord for her supernaturally locating the exact special ring she had wanted. However, when our excitement wore off, I again wondered about cost, but for the size she chose I was astonished at how little it set us back. I immediately reimbursed Mia for this precious stone that was more about her desire being fulfilled than the ring's value.

On a side note, I use *we* when recounting Mia's and my walk with each other—and Jesus—so where you would think I am talking about just the two of us, in my mind I am referring to *we* as myself, Mia, *and* Jesus. From the day Mia introduced herself to me by popping my *Better Together* bracelet (that we both got at Grace Family Church), I knew any future relationship between her and me could only be accomplished through Christ, in Christ, and for Christ.

During the next few weeks, Mia and I spent a couple evenings together when her boys were at their father's. A few other evenings I hung out with Blake, and about one night per week Mia had me stop by when the boys were home. I would usually also see them Saturday evenings at church. Her sons could tell we had become something more than just friends, but we remained discreet, so they had no idea we were discussing marriage. That was hard because I chose to love those boys before I ever met them: you may remember I committed to love any children the Lord brought into my life through a wife—whether my own kids or not—His will be done. Always. Regardless, the more I got around her boys, the greater my love for them grew.

As Mia and I continued becoming closer to each other and our Heavenly Father, we were also planning the wedding. She wanted a very special celebration and because she would be my bride, I was again on board with whatever her heart desired. We chose Sixto and Susan to marry us, our wonderful husband-and-wife leadership team for Thursday night Bible studies at TCF.

While visiting me at Blake's house one evening, Mia and I stood in his backyard on the Hillsborough River and thought it an excellent location for a marriage ceremony. He has a beautiful half acre on the water with huge trees providing plenty of shade from Florida's summer sun. We discussed how it would be perfect for holding baptisms after the wedding, and that led us into the invitation list. We also talked about food for the reception, which Mia pictured as a flavorful and amply flowered Hawaiian luau. "Coincidentally," one of my seafood customers was a locally renowned chef who specializes in that cuisine.

Unfortunately, though, considering the per-person cost of a Hawaiian reception, our guest list quickly grew out of control for our budget. And that was even while avoiding alcohol costs. Neither of us judge friends and family who have a beer, cocktail, or glass of wine from time to time, but we wanted no appearance of hypocrisy on our part since I and Mia were recovering addicts (intravenous drugs and alcohol, respectively). Besides, this would be a celebration done our and the Lord's way, so alcohol did not seem appropriate for a celebration where Mia and I would be presenting ourselves before God and asking His blessing.

We soon realized the wedding cost was becoming unrealistic: it would be virtually impossible to put out that much money over the next three months. Of course, all things are possible for believers, so you might expect that God somehow "pulled out His wallet" and paid for hundreds of guests (causing the money to show up as He had before). While I could see Him showing off like that, this time our Heavenly Father had something different in mind for our wedding, another demonstration of how God lights our paths when we stay obedient to His will and Word.

I'll get to it in a bit.

21

"Way More Than a Ring"

From the excellent job God supplied me, we saved enough to call about a setting for Mia's diamond—more uncharted waters for both of us. For some time already, the jeweler Mia called had been expecting her to contact him (because of his relationship with Marcos). He vowed to make the setting that her heart desired. Mia made the appointment, which would be an added expense to our somewhat lavish wedding plans, all of which was putting my stomach in knots. My fear meter spiked further from Mia's pictures of what looked like an expensive ring with *lots* of diamonds. But again, knowing Who owns all the world's diamonds—no, it's not just De Beers—we knew God would provide if it was meant to be. From all the promises God had already delivered, our faith had been growing exponentially during those months; why would this ring experience be any different?

On a Saturday morning in mid-March, we set out to meet the jeweler at a coffee shop five miles from Mia's home, a trip that would end up being about much more than a ring. On the way, we dropped Blake and Sybil (our future best man and maid of honor) at the airport for their eight-day trip to Israel. They were headed to God's Holy Land as the Lord was about to show up next to a coffeeshop. We got there early and had already had coffee, so we stopped by the Shell gas station next door to pick up a couple energy drinks for the gym later. As we pulled in, Mia saw a black Audi sedan and commented about how pretty it was, so much so that she reiterated her appreciation of it when we came back out of the store. Then as we pulled away, Mia suddenly felt the Holy Spirit say:

"Stop. Go back and look at the license plate."

We backed up and were amazed to see the car's tags had a heart in the middle of the characters "SO8 222." There was that number again and remember that our wedding was potentially set for that year's Day of Pentecost, June 8th. *And* there was a stamp of approval in the upper right corner of the plate: 05-14 (May 14th), Mia's sobriety anniversary. As we were contemplating the meaning, God gave us each this message we repeated in unison:

And the heart seemed to represent God's love for us, ours for Him, and what we have for each other. Besides that, the Lord had been frequently speaking to Mia through hearts. This divine encounter deepened our conviction about how correct those identical bracelets must be, the ones we were wearing when we met; they seemed to have been God's way of declaring that she and I were going to be *better together*—or maybe *better 222 gether.*

And that would not be the only message from the Holy Spirit that morning. Before going in to meet the jeweler, Mia got a perplexed look on her face and told me that the Spirit wanted her to ask this gentleman how he met his wife. With a bit of sarcasm I replied, "Alrighty then." My mind going into this visit had been all about Mia and me, but that mindset keeps people from recognizing when God is trying to show us something about Him. And by this point in our relationship, I was learning not to question when Mia would receive "a word"—communication from above.

The world claims these are just coincidences, and that crediting God is a stretch, but in my mind, much of what I have already mentioned is indisputable, hardcore evidence of God's sovereignty, His divine providence, just like what happened next. Remember that neither of us have met this jeweler before and he has no idea we are Christians. Walking in, we see a man by himself who spots us, gets up, and walks over to greet us. As we head to his table, Mia can't wait so she asks:

"I'm sorry if you find this strange, but I believe I'm supposed to ask how you met your wife."

He light-heartedly replied:

"Which one?"

Not really knowing—but trusting the One who does—Mia quickly added:

"The one you are married to now."

The guy immediately lit up as he began a remarkable story about what happened on an evening five years prior when a female friend invited him to a sushi party where one of her girlfriends would also be. This close friend of his thought the two might like to meet. He went on to tell how he arrived, walked in the front door, instantly locked eyes with a girl standing right in front of him, and felt an immediate and overwhelming attraction. In fact, he knew she was "the one." Though the story was touching, and we shared that immediate feeling of meeting the one, he had not laid out anything earth shattering—but then Mia did! You should probably sit down for this next part. Somehow, she was much more impressed with his story, judging by her awestruck face. She asked:

"Was this the sushi party at Jen's house?"

Now with a similar look of shock as Mia, he stutteringly confirmed:

"Yes. . .yes. . .it was."

We were all blown away—even before Mia laughed and added:

"I was the one you were supposed to meet that night."

This was the Heavenly Father's choice for our jeweler!! Soon after that God-glorifying twist, we noticed his Bible on the table. Seeing us looking at it, he commented that he never brings it out in public but had felt compelled to that day. We briefly mentioned our faith and assured him the meeting was no coincidence. He wanted to know more, especially since jewelers often try to make their pieces reflect the personalities of the owners. So, we shared some of our testimony, which meant God was again using it to draw another person closer to Him, a process confirmed when talked about having recent doubts in his walk with the Lord. He wanted more proof that God is real and hears our prayers in times of need. Well, he got it, including how he was prompted to bring his Bible to a meeting with people whose whole relationship is God breathed.

What are the chances this coffeeshop encounter would unfold

the way it did five years after that party? With God, of course it would, because situations like this are found all over Scripture, incidents that are not coincidence—in fact, the word *coincidence* has no counterpart in ancient Hebrew. The Bible is abundant with historical examples of God's sovereignty (His divine strategy) and providence (guidance).

From my love of Jesus's parables, I enjoy trying to access the mind of Christ in my attempts at creating modern analogies that might help explain the brilliance of God's mind. I believe it makes Him smile. Conversely, my long football analogy may have somewhat soured your disposition, but even at the risk of compounded injury, I hope to redeem my storytelling with a different comparison you might more appreciate. The previous analogy was meant to show how we can maintain an obedient relationship with the Father, Son, and Holy Spirit through any kind of adversity.

Now I want to analogize proof of a divine sovereignty and providence. If you're familiar with the game of chess, you know the greatest players in the world think two or three moves ahead, calculating all the what-ifs, like what move his opponent might make next if he moves his bishop to here or there. How hard would that be to forecast an answer for the same question about each piece he might want to move? The possibilities become mind boggling. But many who have dedicated their lives to chess have developed an intellect that can quickly see a huge percentage of the future scenarios.

Now, to hopefully make our Heavenly Father smile, here's my analogy to that God-ordained coffeeshop encounter: with humans as chess pieces and the earth being the board, imagine Almighty God squaring off against lowly Lucifer, *the* enemy and prince of this world (who will be in checkmate and then tossed into a lake of fire for all eternity—tough game). Of course, this is no real contest, but how many moves ahead do you think God sees in the lives of every person on the board? It is all of them. For everyone. Wow!

The Lord allows us all freewill, but He already knows what we will each end up doing with it— He's seen the entire future. Regardless, He instructs us to use our present time to make moves that further His kingdom. The Bible's account of Christ's birth well illustrates God's strategy and guidance, His sovereignty and providence had the Lord not directed Caesar Augustus to call for a census, Joseph and Mary would never have traveled to Bethlehem to register themselves, so several moves prior, God clearly put in place His plan to use that emperor for carrying out His will. And the Lord's desire was to have Christ born in an area connected to King David, a place prophesied 700 years earlier through Isaiah 7:13-14:

> *"Hear now, you house of David! Is it not enough to try the patience of humans? Will you try the patience of my God also? Therefore the Lord himself will give you a sign: The virgin will conceive and give birth to a son, and will call Him Immanuel."*

Seven centuries before Jesus was born, God preordained for Jesus to be born in Bethlehem, a little town near Jerusalem that's known as the birthplace of David and the City of David. It is the town where the great prophet Samuel anointed David, revealing God's preordained decision to one day make David a king of Israel. To fulfill God's prophecies of having Jesus come from the line of David and be born in David's city, how many moves ahead—through many, many people—did that take? So, God gives signs, as He told us in Isaiah 14:7:

> *"Therefore the Lord himself will give you a sign. . ."*

Prophecy proves the Bible came from God and is without error, just as you would expect from something the Holy Spirit breathed into men so they would write the books down. The inerrancy of Scripture is proven over and over and over by the Lord's 2500 detailed prophecies, of which 2000 have already come true—and the rest are lining up in these end days. As has been written by many before me, consider that the sixty-six books of the Bible were written by forty authors on three continents in three languages over a period of fifteen hundred years—by men of different educational and societal levels, from fishermen to kings—*yet* all sixty-six have a miraculous unity and agreement. So, the Holy Bible was not something mankind could have ever come up with on their own; it had to be the Holy Spirit writing the Scriptures through all those men.

And it makes sense that God would want to give us His road map for life, so that all would have a chance to be saved and live with their Heavenly Father for eternity. And why wouldn't He want to answer the core questions of life that we all have, like who exactly are we, why are we here, and what brings us joy? In His manual for humans, God gave us the key to having true joy, peace, and love during this life: our fruits of the Spirit increase proportionally to how much of our days we focus on Him and glorify Him as part of a close relationship with Him.

Jesus died for the entire fallen creation—including birds, fish, ants, plants, and us—so it is true that he died for mankind as *part* of creation, but that description is incomplete and can lead to what we have seen over the past 2000 years: a self-focused Christianity that can impede and harm our relationship with God, as well as hinder others from wanting to have a relationship with Him. Yes, Jesus died for you and me, but His greatest priority was to bring glory to God, and that is because our God is the only perfect example of pure truth and love, so we should take every opportunity to credit the Father, Son, and Holy Ghost for every good thing.

So like Jesus demonstrated by going to the unfathomable lengths of dying a horrible death on a cross (firstly, to glorify God by redeeming all creation), we too must lead others in the right direction, which means living an outwardly focused Christian life where we do *all* for the glory of God. That divine directive—to take the focus off ourselves—is what Jesus said when asked to name the greatest commandment. He answered in Mark 12:30–31:

> " 'Love the Lord your God with all your heart and with all
> your soul and with all your mind and with all your strength.'
> The second is this: 'Love your neighbor as yourself.' There is
> no commandment greater than these."

Besides daily doing all for the kingdom of God, as our way to thank Him for saving us, the side benefits for you and me are a greater measure of peace, love, joy, patience, kindness, goodness, faithfulness, gentleness, and self-control. What more could we want. . .other than eternal life? We get that too.

With that in mind, let's give God more glory by examining His divine strategy laid out in chess moves He made nearly six years before this meeting at a coffeeshop in Lutz, Florida. Years earlier, I had lived fifty miles away, but then became a homeless addict who landed at the ARC rehab program, where I met the woman who would be the reason for the ring meeting. That's just a couple moves God made with me. On top of that are Mia's connections and ours together.

Hopefully all this inspires you to look back at how God's divine strategy has been part of your own life, as one of His highly prized, precious chess pieces. I marvel at how eternity for each of us was planned even before our all-knowing Chess Master knitted us together in our mothers' wombs. *Every* person He ever brings into the world has been created for something wonderful. We only need to step into our place on God's chessboard and let Him know we're open to whatever moves He desires. Then we will truly share the Apostle Paul's view: to live is Christ and to die is gain.

And part of our future will be sharing in God's victory on that preordained day when our King of kings and Lord of lords ends His long suffering, having waited patiently for thousands of years so that more people have a chance to choose Jesus, instead of rejecting Him and ending up with the enemy. That day Christ will declare "checkmate" against that evil entity and his demons who have tortured our world.

As promised, this chapter has been about *way* more than a ring. It's been about the sovereignty of our King.

22

"Our Plans or His?"

"Happy wife, happy life" is a valid saying, and I try following Christ's example in protecting and serving the one I love. Sometimes that means taking a backseat, especially when that person has grandiose ideas for the perfect wedding ceremony and reception, the sort of desires a wise man would do well to help her fulfill. As early as she can understand, a little girl is taught to believe some honorable, handsome prince—who had always been meant for her—will one day ride a beautiful white stallion into her life, sweep her up, and take her off to his magical kingdom. There the two will live happily ever after. . .but not until she gets the perfect wedding day!

I would soon be marrying a true Proverbs 31 wife, a woman of noble character. And I can assure you she did not reach that biblical status overnight. Like all who strive to do God's will, becoming very much like Jesus is an extremely long process, because—unlike Him—every human is born depraved, as Jeremiah 17:9 tells us:

> "The human heart is the most deceitful of all things, and desperately wicked."

But for us and for all who despair, we must remember that the Lord hasn't brought us this far in life to leave us where we are now. Like everyone else, Mia and I were born with deceit in our hearts, so we each needed much growth through reading God's Word and seeking a closer relationship with Him. This learning over time helps all of us better recognize whether we are truly pursuing God's plan—or ours. As we live more and more for Christ, supernatural revelations can happen, like what God did with that coffeeshop meeting. Then these sorts of wonders cause fallible humans to overreach and feel like we have the whole God thing figured out, but we must maintain humility, let go, lean on God, and have Him continue leading however *He* chooses. The Lord has it fully figured out—we certainly do not, and we will be discovering the mind of God for eternity.

A few weeks later in March 2014, our best man and maid of honor experienced that amazing trip to Israel's Holy Land, a trip worthy of its own book. Meanwhile we were working toward fulfilling Mia's desire for a substantial wedding with over sixty on the guest list so far, as well as a couple bridesmaids and groomsmen. Because our focus was to demonstrate marriage done God's way, we were excited to share the ceremony with as many as possible, but we did not have the money—at least I didn't.

As I mentioned, Mia envisioned a catered Hawaiian luau, and the list would probably end up at about seventy-five people in Blake's riverside backyard. Her initial decoration would be purple and white orchids garnishing the guest plates, and then build from there. In this celebration of what God put together (Mia and me), she wanted to go all out, making our God-ordained event something to remember. And as I have tried to do for the rest of our lives since, I wanted to protect, honor, and serve the one God chose for me to love. This means selflessly trying to fulfill her heart's desires. But through all these plans, that core question kept surfacing in my mind: were these *our* plans or *His*?

All this led to a defining moment in our relationship. My fiancée wanted a fairytale wedding and I was feeling extremely inadequate from not being able to afford it. Mia's thinking was that God knew the desires of her heart, so if she was the one for me, the Lord would provide everything she and I needed to have the wedding she envisioned—and maybe that meant we should postpone the wedding until we could save enough to have the ceremony and reception the Lord had shown her.

Talk of postponement took more wind out of my sails, leaving us at a daunting hurdle: I desperately wanted to give Mia her heart's desires, but our financial situation meant there was no way for that to happen in just two months. With that dilemma, of course delay would come up, but we had both agreed that God gave us a wedding date of June 8th. Would we push aside Pentecost? Did it matter to anyone? What do we do? Tensions were running high as Mia's birthday approached; discord grew, and the wheels were coming off our Salvation Army bus; now even our relationship appeared as if it might be up the Hillsborough River without a paddle (actually, in flat Florida that is not much of an issue). Growing extremely frustrated, I finally challenged Mia:

"Are these our plans, or His. . .God's wedding, or ours?"

Mia had a financially difficult childhood and adolescence, but her lifestyle as a mature young woman and then mother had continuously improved over the years. She was *not* spoiled but had become financially comfortable and was used to acquiring what she wanted. Had I met her years earlier when I was at the top of my secular-business game, affording worldly provisions for her would not have been a problem, but after having become homeless, penniless, jobless, and addicted to prescription drugs, I was far from the abundant provider it seemed Mia might need for her happiness.

Recounting all those mental machinations, can you see how we humans are easily trapped into trying to provide joy for others? But only God gives that. All this wedding turmoil was leading to an important lesson for Mia and me: God had put us together on a righteous path that would bring glory to His kingdom, but near that sort of power, human pride is always lurking. Mia became convinced that a fairytale wedding would fulfill God's promises to her, and I had become driven by the worldly gauge of success, judging myself by the size of my bank account. How else could I provide my fiancée's desires? Even after months of studying God's Word, this struggle during our engagement convinced me that more money would make Mia happy, meaning the enemy had gotten a solid foothold in our relationship. So, all we could do at that point was to step back, let go, let God, and wait on Him to say whether we had been wrongly following our plans or rightly seeking His.

Through the tension, we continued getting together for Thursday night Bible studies, church on the weekends, and dinner Sunday nights with Mia's boys. She wanted me to know them, but remained somewhat guarded, and I didn't blame her. Now that she was two years clean and sober, Mia's rededication to the Lord had grown so foundational that the boys were finally confident she would not be going back to her old ways. She was a great mom whose walk with the Lord definitely impacted her boys, but they had been through a lot, so they certainly did not need an upset mom—or a negative influence dropping by.

Soon Mia's ring was ready. Though I had made a month of payments, the jeweler was getting impatient for the final one, as was Mia. I was doing my best after giving ill-advised promises— God had done amazing work pulling me out of the muck and mire, planting my feet on solid rock, and putting a new song in my mouth—but financially I wasn't where I needed to be after making Mia assurances that I would be able to support her two sons, her home, and her. I could not even pay off the engagement ring, so how was Mia going to trust me with even more substantial responsibilities? This dilemma is addressed in Matthew 25:23 where

Jesus tells another of His wonderful parables. This one is about how God trusts us with small things until we prove our faithfulness and are granted greater responsibility:

> "His master replied, 'Well done, good and faithful servant! You have been faithful with a few things; I will put you in charge of many things. Come and share your master's happiness!' "

During this time there was *no* sharing in my Master's happiness: pre-wedding days were flying by with expenses mounting. For Mia's birthday on April 9th, I was not even able to take her and her sons out for dinner. Because of the money I owed Blake, the cost of the ring, and my car situation, it was all I could do to afford bare necessities. Again, Mia was not spoiled, but she was used to getting what she desired, so I was clearly falling short and could see her disappointment. Sensing something was amiss, I was certainly remorseful for making empty promises. My heart's desire was to make good on my commitments, which included giving her what *I* thought was right. But Proverbs 14:12 puts that idea into perspective:

> "There is a way that seems right to a man, but in the end it leads to death."

Feeling this turmoil deep in my spirit, I knew it would take a God-sized miracle to move forward into what He had shown us, so I went to my knees, praying like never before that God would lift Mia and cleanse me of any unrighteousness still abounding in my heart. I knew who she was in Christ and that she was the one for me, but this was a time when both of us had to learn that *our* plans were not *His*. In fact, looking back now, it's hard to believe how selfish we both had been, especially for two people spending so much time together in God's Word.

Here's Mia with more about that—and she actually agrees with me.

Mia
• • • • • • •

I hate to admit it, but Robby was right. We were *both* selfish. And that was while God had been continuously showing me His glory and sovereignty through some attention-grabbing doves that the Lord spread over a long period of time leading up to my April 2014 birthday.

One day well before meeting Robby, while driving through the alleyway behind my local Publix grocery store, I came to a halt for an oddly placed stop sign. Before I could let off the brake, a bird suddenly flew down and landed right in front of my car. Not wanting to hit the little thing— which appeared to be a white dove—waiting to see it safely leave. I thought it odd that I had not seen a white dove in the wild before and this one had strangely perfect timing. After the cooing creature kept me waiting for at least a minute, walking back and forth beside and in front of my car, the Holy Spirit led me to understand that this winged visitor was symbolic of holiness and marriage.

I had done a lot of praying on that subject for my best friend Valerie, so this encounter felt like a sign *for her.* For me, life was fulfilling with just God and my boys. My relationship with the Lord meant walking closely with the lover of my soul. Valerie on the other hand was single, and she desired a family of her own. It was not uncommon for God to speak to me in such a way, so once the dove departed, I called her right away to explain what the Spirit had just shown me and how it might mean she would soon meet the man God had for her.

Not long after that first conspicuous dove, as I was walking out of Tampa's International Mall, a second white dove flew down and landed beside me. Again, I stopped and stared in amazement as it walked all around me. I knew it was another sign about marriage and holiness. From seeing this second pure-white dove in such a short period—after I had not seen one in the wild my entire life—I began to think these messages from God might be for me.

This was also the time where I was open to God restoring my marriage. And besides these doves, the Holy Spirit had been impressing upon me to act as a wife and mother. Because I was single, this seems to mean keeping myself unavailable for dating. Also, my relationship with the children's father had been amicable. With all that in mind, I was hopeful for restoration, yet perplexed at how God might make that happen when he was in a committed relationship.

I know this reconciliation scenario sounds crazy, but when you are closely seeking God's will, life does not always make sense to our mortal minds. In fact, the Scriptures talk about the Lord's people often being ridiculed for what appeared to be radical obedience. Being willing to follow whatever God chooses for your life is always the best practice, but it often requires keeping strong faith through unpredictable requests, believing what the eyes cannot see nor the mind understand. Even though the dove incidents were months before I met Robby, total obedience had become the story of my life, so I did not question God on the matter. And I knew He would continue confirming His desires for me through more signs and my time in His Word, so I waited with eager anticipation for what might come next.

But I was completely unprepared for what God sent my way: a case of girl meeting boy in an otherworldly, divine connection. Shortly after the Holy Spirit introduced Robby to me, I was reminded of the two doves and decided to wait on the Lord's third confirmation. Still today, God seems to give me signs in strings of three, a significant number seen in the Bible 467 times, including the Trinity, Jonah being three days in the belly of the whale, Jesus spending three days inside the earth, and our Savior praying three times at Gethsemane.

As single people, both Robby and I had made a commitment to forgo dating relationships so we could focus on God. But the Lord seemed to be drawing us closer to each other. And this led to issues about how close we should become: neither of us were willing to compromise on godly behavior, so living or sleeping together was out of the question. But because of that commitment, it was apparent that our quickly progressing relationship would have to reach marriage—or end. And I wasn't even sure I *wanted* marriage. Besides that, the circumstances of our lives were not what I would have imagined for a relationship that I would want to take far. Still, just as I am today, back then I was willing to put God's will above my own, open to trusting in His sovereignty over my life.

Keeping all that in mind, you can probably understand our childlike faith and curiosity when driving down the interstate one day, talking about potential wedding dates—*if* we were to get married. I mentioned how symbolic Pentecost had been in my life, so for kicks and giggles we Googled what that special day would fall on for 2014. There on the calendar square we came face to face with a white dove symbolizing that year's Day of Pentecost, June 8th. I thought:

Could this be the third white dove, the confirmation I have been waiting for?

It might seem so to those reading this, but something inside me said to seek further confirmation. Excited *and* skeptical, my response was that God would confirm that date *if* it was His will for us to marry. So, we waited with eager anticipation for more of the Lord's will to be revealed— we were on a sort of Holy Spirit scavenger hunt for revelations. Our job was to prayerfully seek and recognize His will; then be obedient to it.

Partially because so much time had passed since that second white dove in the mall parking lot— before even meeting Robby—my faith in God wanting me and Robby together was being continually tested, including from my pride and a spirit of fear. Our relationship was beginning to lose the battle. Reality was hitting more and more each day with the depravity of our situation while we had a quickly approaching wedding date of June 8th. We were best friends, but I wondered whether that was all we were intended to be. Was all this we had been experiencing actually from God? Or was it just coincidence? I was desperate to hear from my Lord. In my mind, the rapidly worsening situation needed a huge intervention, if we were to keep my and Robby's relationship going. In fact, I was *once again* ready to throw in the towel because of how difficult it had become. And I had two teenage boys to raise. They needed a mom—not a mother and her homeless husband!

So, my spirit felt these dove sightings were confirmation of the wedding date, and I expected to see more, but my close walk with the Lord had taught me that something as huge as marriage would surely involve a much more substantial sign. Smaller signs with doves had been showing up during Robby's and my time together, like an encounter when Robby went with me to get the weekly groceries. We were walking down an aisle when I noticed a store employee with tattoos on his arms. After looking at the shelves for a moment, I felt led to ask him if I could see them. He happily obliged and told us how he had let the artist decide what to draw with a couple of them, and then he flipped his arm over to reveal another that he said he had drawn himself. It was a huge dove! Robby and I turned to each other and smiled.

By the Holy Spirit I knew this was confirmation of being on track, but *if* I were really "the one" for Robby, God would make that abundantly obvious. This incident had not been it. Numerous confirming signs continued daily, like some song at an interesting moment, many Rhema Words (words spoken out loud by the Holy Spirit) heard while in the Scriptures, a billboard, a phone call, butterflies, ladybugs, and other "coincidental" items appearing out of nowhere. The timing of everything was too precise to be happenstance. I wanted so desperately to believe, but I was afraid.

Then something else miraculous occurred that was similar to me finding that white handbag with pink hearts in my closet. While praying, the Lord led me to walk into my bedroom and open a drawer that contained a locked jewelry box. I hadn't opened it for quite a while but remembering my previous prompting when I found that book in the mystery purse, I opened it with high expectations and was not disappointed. Waiting for me was a tiny white dove with a bit of sky blue—heaven blue—painted on its wings.

God's overwhelming presence surrounded me as I was awestruck. Though something still felt a bit off, I knew I was close to where He wanted me. Also, positive and interesting was that shade of blue on the dove's wings. In recent days while Robby and I had been discussing the wedding, I would see that particular blue in my mind. I was excited and determined to find out why. God had apparently dropped that mystery dove in my jewelry box, a claim that sounds ridiculous to many, but the same could be said for our Heavenly Father's many other miracles: He rained down manna (food) for the desert-dwelling Israelites; delivered the bound, sick, brokenhearted, and deformed; walked on water and turned it into wine; parted the Red Sea; and even brought the dead to life. I have learned not to question what or how God does His business; I only know that He will reveal more to me as I continue seeking Him and studying His Word.

As a Florida hurricane of emotional ups and downs were approaching Robby's and my relationship, I *knew* inside that this dove was not the marriage-confirming wonder I had been waiting for. You may be wondering how many more signs I needed to confirm Robby's claim that I am *the one*? Well, that number had to be enough for me to *know* it was God's will! While so many aspects of our journey together with God seemed to be falling in place, doubts about whether I should marry Robby were getting continually stronger. Were they from the enemy? Maybe I was losing it. What was wrong? I loved Robby and we were close to being engaged but was still feeling like he did not meet my standards for a husband.

This came to an agonizing head on my forty-first birthday when the worry made me sick to my stomach. I had been obsessing on the potential problems with marrying a man who had no home and could not even afford a birthday dinner out, one that my boys would expect to have with me. A quickly approaching marriage meant his wedding-ring payments were too high. The only way he had been able to take me out was if I paid. Though that certainly sounds selfish on my part since the ring was for me, I had two boys to protect. They and I had been through a lot of turmoil at *my* hands, and now that the Lord had delivered us, I would not take the chance of reverting to any semblance of that struggle. Besides, I was fine with just God and me.

The internal conversation and resulting stress brought me to a breaking point. I could no longer go through with the wedding, at least not with a date that gave me little chance to see whether Robby would get completely back on his feet. Needing a break from all the noise in my mind, I headed to the facility where Robby and I had been leading addicts in the *Recovery in Christ* program. I had to drop some items off anyway and knew the building would be empty, so this would be a way to isolate in the presence of God, seeking His will with no distractions.

In a perfect world my future fiancé would have made plans for us to do something special with the boys. But since that was not the case, and even though I recognized how *my* heart was not right, I battled all day in the throne room of God, praying intensely while groaning from emotional pain. On my birthday I was obligated to be with my boyfriend, and he would certainly want to be with me. But because Robby had made no plans for my children, the only solution seemed to be leaving Robby out, which would be wrong and severely hurt his feelings. With all the anxiety of no apparent solution, after a while I just wanted to stay home and hide under the covers until that day passed. The situation turned into a messed up, difficult day of me relentlessly imploring the Lord for help.

While away talking with God at the facility, I read Scripture, prayed, cried, groaned, worshiped, and did everything I could to shake the disappointment and despair—to no avail. Not finding relief, I came home where Robby had been waiting at my house. In hopes of keeping busy to prevent a contentious conversation, I went straight for a closet to clean. How crazy is that?! Most women have done that a time or two. Looking back, I would have handled it all differently, but at that time I was not willing to wait, pay attention, and yield to God's help. Instead, this birthday issue was supplying me with a false justification to throw a full-on spiritual tantrum. And I normally cared little about my birthdays; that is, until my boyfriend could not meet my expectations.

Understandably, Robby did not permit me to hide long in the closet. He was deeply concerned about my behavior and desperate to find out what was wrong. I knew he felt my displeasure in him, and then I made matters worse by not communicating. But how was I going to complain that he could not even take me and the boys out to dinner? How silly would that sound? Here was a godly man who was truly doing everything he could—and then some—to stay surrendered to God. Like me, he had not been willing to get ahead of the Lord's plans for his life; in fact, Robby could have gone straight back to a career with the amazing financial success he had prior to addiction, but we both knew that was not where God wanted him. The daily efforts and desires from both of us were obedient to whatever the Lord allowed and prescribed, no matter what.

Again, I knew I was being ridiculous, but I could not contain myself. A deceptive thought process had captured my mind, emotions, and will. I wanted the feelings to stop, but in reality, all along throughout our relationship, something deep inside had doubted Robby was the right one for me. Through all my new-found hope, faith, and trust in God, I had been challenging Him about the relationship with Robby—even though the Lord confirmed my correct path *over and over and over*. But I would not divorce again. Marriage would be for life, a God-ordained union. So, I was seeking more and more assurance, especially since I already had real joy through my close walk with Jesus.

My tormenting worries persisted about a potential future with some broke, homeless addict. The Lord's many signs to the contrary were not enough to temper my growing conviction that rushing into marriage with Robby might be the worst mistake of my life—and I had made some horrible decisions. We moved to the kitchen table where tears were rolling down both of our faces as Robby struggled to understand. I could barely get the words out, but finally confessed that I could no longer be in a relationship with him. Trying to help, I added that the fears, doubts, and pressures of a June wedding had become too much, so I needed to postpone indefinitely.

After a minute where both of us were speechless and I firmed my resolve, the doorbell rang.

With both of us a hot mess, I had no intention of answering and asked Robby to ignore it. Probably from not knowing what else to do, he got up anyway and went to the front door. There was Valerie. Seeing Robby's face, she walked right in, looked at me, and asked what was wrong. I was not able to answer. What could I say? That I'm a brat? Would I explain how this grown woman was throwing a tantrum and ending a relationship with the guy I love because he can't take me and my boys to dinner?

That would have been the truth and I was sure this revelation would launch Valerie into fix-it mode or at least into trying to help with the fallout. But she was too excited to even address our life-changing issue. While Robby and I sat there staring at her with an advanced level of shock, she blurted out a disclosure that had been coming for weeks:

"Mia, I have been holding something for you, waiting for the right time. I do not know what is going on with you two, and I can't explain why, but while home just now I got the feeling that now was the right moment, so I came right over. It might help. Before I show you though, let me tell you how I got it."

Valerie went on to explain how—weeks earlier—she and our friend Abigail were having a Bible study while Valerie was taking care of a special-needs woman named Liza. At one point when Valerie was across the room, Abigail handed Liza what appeared to be a small trinket, so Valerie walked over to see what it was. Abigail did not know why the urge had come over her to hand Liza her favorite piece of jewelry. It had been in her possession for years. As Valerie saw what it was, she knew the unfortunate truth that because of Liza's condition, this special item would mostly likely end up lost. And when Valerie took a look, she knew the gift was ultimately meant for me. Valerie explained the issue with Liza and asked Abigail if she could give the jewelry to someone God had planned for it. Abigail happily agreed.

Valerie had been waiting for the Holy Spirit's prompting, which came just before she was obedient to visit my house that day—thank God! Before Abigail, Liza, Valerie, Robby, and I were born, the Lord knew exactly what would transpire on my forty-first birthday, because He orchestrates the coordinated steps of His children. God had constructed an elaborate lesson for me, while plopping in a few other people who would be witnesses to His glory—including the man I truly loved and still do today. I had only needed to get my emotions out of the way and let the Holy Spirit lead.

Valerie reached forward and opened her hand to reveal the dove I had been waiting for. There was no human explanation possible. This precisely timed—down to the minute—supernatural development gave me undeniable assurance that my godly, homeless, Salvation Army man (with the Mercedes hooptie that was at least better than his previous junker) was the one God picked out for me.

A year before meeting Robby, I had rededicated my life to Jesus. And during the days that followed, the Lord sent me hearts: like when He supernaturally placed the book *When a Woman Discovers Her Dream* in a heart-covered bag on the top shelf of my bedroom closet. Now well into my time with Robby, here was Valerie opening her palm to display that dove necklace that was divinely placed so I would see it. God's timing is *always* perfect; we just need to build a relationship with Him, so we discover *His* plan for our lives, instead of only following *our* often-sketchy ideas.

Now I want to turn the writing back over to Robby so he can tell you the rest of our story—the Lord's story—starting with the end of this chapter.

Robby
· · · · · · · ·

I've learned that Christians can study Scripture for decades and still have blind spots; we are always learning more about the mind of God and will for eternity—how cool is that! And if those around us do not lovingly point out our shortcomings, we will continue trying to remove specks from others' eyes while ignoring the logs in our own. Even when others do mention our faults—and are right—pride causes us to deny the accusation as groundless or justify our involvement and then continue being deceived. Fortunately, Mia and I knew that God's playbook for humanity has the answers for all issues of human frailty, so we decided to put *our* wedding plans on hold and lean into the Bible for *His* wedding plans. In John 16:33, Jesus reassures us that He is the key to survive *anything* this life throws at us:

> *"In this world you will have troubles, but take "heart" for I have overcome the world."*

We needed Scripture to find our *bridge over troubled waters*. There is *nothing* like Scripture for providing truthful ways to bridge the gap between issues like sorrow and joy, war and peace, foolishness and wisdom, and discord versus love and respect. Diligent study of the Word helps us learn whether our plans are His—or just ours.

23

"Turning the Corner Through God's Word"

Though we had put the majority of what God showed us into *our* plans, we failed at fully making them *His* plans. But fallible humans learn by trial and error: sometimes we sail out of port in the right direction and then circumstances blow us off course, a reality that ended up sidelining *our* wedding plans so we could lean into God's Word for direction. We needed to wait on God while getting back to the basics of our Christian walk with Him.

During this time, Mia and I were facilitating *Recovery in Christ* meetings at TCF, a twelve-step Jesus-centered program. We allowed the Holy Spirit to lead our group, while constantly researching Scripture for passages that would encourage attendees. I think Mia and I benefited the most, especially from these sorts of promises from God:

> *"For I know the plans I have for you, declares the Lord, plans to prosper you and not to harm you, plans to give you hope and a future."*
> (Jeremiah 29:11)

> *"All a person's ways seem pure to them, but motives are weighed by the Lord."*
> (Proverbs 16:2)

> *"Call to me. . .and I will show you great and mighty things, which you do not know."*
> (Jeremiah 33:3)

Mia and I attempted a purely biblical approach to the wedding, but only the Lord knows if our motives were all godly. We sought His guidance, and He was faithful to answer, so circumstances could not fully blow us off course from God's will. During that trying time, He gave us all the Bible research for class to help us adjust the sails and stay more on course.

After Mia's birthday, God showed up in a way only He can. It happened through our willingness to obey His Word and give Him the glory whenever we witness His signs, miracles, and wonders. In fact, this entire book has been written to display His glory. Again, when Mia's ring was finished, the jeweler was looking for final payment, and knowing how our testimony had made a profound impact on him, I did not want him to believe we were hypocrites—action speaks louder than preaching. All of us become guilty of hypocrisy at some point, but Luke 12:48 calls Christians to a higher standard:

> *"From everyone who has been given much, much will be demanded; and from the one who has been entrusted with much, much more will be asked."*

My financial back was against the wall, having exhausted my financial resources but needing to come up with $1200. So, I hit my knees, just as I had been every morning since getting saved, a show of gratitude for another day serving my Savior; at the risk of sounding boastful, the truth is that I would spend all day walking around on my knees (in submission to the Father) just from recognizing my endless need for His amazing grace and mercy.

Here I was a few days after Mia's birthday, having exhausted my financial resources but needing over a thousand dollars. You may have guessed that my next move was down a tried-and-true road: my best buddy Blake. One day during dinner (before our usual evening watching sermons and studying God's Word), I expressed my concern about paying off Mia's ring. You may remember that Mia and I had dropped Blake and Sybil at the airport as they were traveling to Israel on the same morning we met with the jeweler. I told Blake about the incredible revelations that took place at the coffee shop, how our testimony seemed to make an impact on the jeweler, how I had already made sizable payments, and that the ring maker now wanted the rest of his money. As soon as Blake understood the potential hypocrisy from me continuing to drag my feet, he volunteered to loan the money if I would allow the ring to be kept in his safe until it was fully paid off.

Once again, God stepped up in our time of need. No, I am not saying Blake is God, *though* He is a servant of the Lord, one who is sensitive to the Spirit and responds without questioning. Through my spiritual and financial issues (as I turned my circumstances around), I saw Blake repeat his godly service over and over and over. He was often the answer from God when I remained obedient to Matthew 7:7–8:

> *"Ask and it will be given to you; seek and you will find; knock and the door will be opened to you. For everyone who asks receives; the one who seeks finds; and to the one who knocks, the door will be opened."*

Help from God's servant and steady study of the Scriptures had continuously corrected my course through the ongoing financial struggles. I was finally able to call the jeweler, pay off the ring, and take possession. I would soon see it put safely away in Blake's safe, but before that I called Mia on the way home because I wanted her to see her ring and make sure it fit properly. After paying Blake back, I would be able to propose, and it would be hers to keep. We met, Mia tried on her beautiful black-diamond engagement ring, and I left with a smile on my face, knowing God's plans were coming together.

The next day was a normally unwelcome date for many Americans, but for me April 15th, 2014, marked the first milestone anniversary of old friends pulling me back from the cliff's edge—I had fully intended to end my life. Going from that to a year clean and sober was special and would not have been possible without Jesus at the center of my recovery; I had failed a few times under my own strength. Philippians 4:13 describes the reason for my recent success:

"I can do all things through Christ who gives me strength."

Around this time something else came full circle: Mia's North Carolina trip that past Thanksgiving, and specifically the day she saw that large window full of newspaper articles that included one about the coming four blood moons. Bible prophecy makes up over one-fourth of all Scripture, yet few churches teach on it today, resulting in over 65% of Christians not fully trusting their Bible. But prophecy provides irrefutable proof that the Scriptures were given to us by the Holy Spirit writing those books through men. On his best day, by himself man cannot pull off even a few specific predictions of the future, let alone 2000 that have been 100% accurate.

The Bible's end-times prophecy (eschatology) appears in Old Testament chapters like Daniel 12, Zechariah 12, and Joel 2. As far as the New Testament, Jesus speaks about the final days in Matthew 24 and so does John throughout Revelation. For Mia's and my story, I want to mention the New Testament eschatology of Acts 2:17–21 where Peter tells the crowd what Old Testament prophet Joel disclosed:

> *"In the last days, God says, I will pour out my Spirit on all people. Your sons and daughters will prophesy, your young men will see visions, your old men will dream dreams. Even on my servants, both men and women, I will pour out my Spirit in those days, and they will prophesy. I will show wonders in the heavens above and signs on the earth below, blood and fire and billows of smoke. The sun will be turned to darkness and the moon to blood before the coming of the great and glorious day of the Lord. And everyone who calls on the name of the Lord will be saved."*

This profound passage mentions wonders in the heavens, like the blood moons Mia read about in the headlines of that article. These sorts of signs are part of God's divine strategy that has been playing out to perfection for 6000 years. As a side note, God's eyewitness of creation in Genesis tells us our planet and universe are only *thousands* of years old. Evolution is bad science, it's not scientific theory, it's a bankrupt guess, the Bible's history is true, and that means we have a young earth. Most dating methods show a young earth—except for a very flawed few that are endlessly cited. So, whenever you hear or read someone claiming "millions" or "billions" of years, realize they might as well be saying, "long, long ago and far, far away..."

Like God finishing the heavens and earth in *six days,* His plan for man's *six thousand years* on this planet are about over; any day now all believers will be raptured off the earth to meet Jesus in the sky. So as an incentive for Christians to use the little time we have left to glorify God—by witnessing for Jesus—I want to mention what *unbelievers* must be saved from, a horrific time that Bible prophecy warns about, and it will be starting soon! But to keep the flow of our story, we are putting that information in an addendum at the back of this book.

And as part of God's plans, Mia and I are surrendered vessels being led by our faith—not our sight—two people completely onboard with His will being done instead of ours. Getting back to my first anniversary of being clean and sober, the day before, on April 14th, God solved my predicament of needing $1200 for the jeweler. Blake was again the obedient servant, I got the ring, and I was even able to show Mia.

Once home, I began counting down to my official anniversary at midnight. That time would also begin a total lunar eclipse—the first of those four blood moons Mia had read about. The eclipse was set to reach totality at 3am on April 15th. Around 11pm I prayed with Mia, and we said goodnight. I got in bed and was trying to fall asleep when the Holy Spirit suddenly prompted me to write another poem. Here is what I wrote on my cellphone and then texted to Mia just after midnight:

Wake Me at Three to See God's Glory

As for now, I'm fast asleep in my bed,
awakened at three to a moon that's blood red.
What an awesome sight for millions to behold,
the first of four as this story unfolds.

A biblical sign the end grows near,
we welcome the Messiah's return with love and not fear.
Be patient my brothers there are three more to go,
many signs, miracles, and wonders He still wants to show.

It's in the good book for those to find,
Ask and ye shall receive as God summons your mind.
Salvation awaits those who still have doubt,
for God's grace and mercy never run out.

So let tonight's blood moon speak to your heart,
for His love is real and will never depart.

Now rest my dear brothers from this wonder you've seen,
as God's glorious blood moon regains its bright sheen.

And soon it will set, the cycle will be over,
as we wait for the second to appear in early October.
Until then, pay attention and be faithful in prayer,
as the Lord reveals more signs, miracles, and wonders for
believers who care!

This may sound hard to believe, but after finishing the poem and falling asleep, my eyes sprang open at the exact time that blood-moon eclipse reached its totality, and it hung in the exact middle of my bedroom window, just like the St. Augustine cross Mia and I saw at the center of the motel window when we opened the drapes of room 222.

And now here I was staring at my first total lunar eclipse, and it happened to be the first of four blood moons that were set to come, a celestial phenomenon the Bible describes as a wondrous sign from heaven. Excited enough to disregard the wee hour of the morning, I knocked on Blake's bedroom door, letting him know we must go outside to witness God's wonders.

Standing there at 3am staring at the sky, I brought out the poem God inspired me to write at the start of the eclipse. While we witnessed the first of those four blood moons, I began to recite the poem: "Wake me at three to see God's glory. . ." Remember, Blake's house is where my journey began exactly one year earlier when he took me to the Salvation Army ARC program that saved my life and eternal soul. Here we were back at his house where God was having Blake witness all this firsthand. The Lord was using my mess to send a message: Blake saw Jesus open my eyes to the truth and set me free. I believe God used me to show Blake that anyone's course can be corrected through God's Word.

24

"Straight to the Cross"

Our relationship troubles seemed to get more difficult as we closed in on the wedding day— whatever God unites, the devil wants to divide—and I believe the enemy attacked us more because the chosen day was Pentecost. Even before marriage, Mia and I had become a significant threat to the kingdom of darkness, and that might sound boastful, but consider what Paul said in 2 Corinthians 11:30–33 after listing a myriad of trials and tribulations he endured:

> "If I must boast, I will boast of the things that show my weakness. The God and Father of the Lord Jesus, who is to be praised forever, knows that I am not lying. In Damascus the governor under King Aretas had the city of Damascenes guarded in order to arrest me. But I was lowered in a basket from a window in the wall and slipped through his hands."

Our story has been one of weakness: two extremely broken people from different walks of life who, like the Apostle Paul, surrendered all to Jesus. Then through God's divine sovereignty and providence, He had our paths cross and revealed His plans for us to help His kingdom together. Now nine months later the two of us were two months from becoming one on the same day the Holy Spirit indwelled His first 3000 people:

> "When the day of Pentecost came, they were all together in one place. Suddenly a sound like the blowing of a violent wind came from heaven and filled the whole house where they were sitting. They saw what seemed to be tongues of fire that separated and came to rest on each of them. All of them were

filled with the Holy Spirit and began to speak in other tongues as the Spirit enabled them."
(Acts 2:1–2)

Especially because we chose Pentecost for the wedding, the devil's attacks increased as we approached our ceremony meant to glorify God. Both of us were walking more and more by faith, and less and less by sight, moving forward together in the full authority of who we were created to be in Christ. This enraged the enemy, but through that persecution our Heavenly Father was leading us straight to the cross. So, the devil would have to get over this loss, just like the multitude of other failures he has had throughout history.

Think about the Bible's account of Gideon and his relatively tiny army of 300 men. Even though he was facing a force of 120,000, God had him drastically decrease his army to the insurmountable odds of 400 to 1. The Lord orchestrates the most unlikely outcomes, using the least expected people. Then the Holy Spirit leads the underdog to a victory that can only be seen as supernatural, meaning God gets the glory for the win; thus, we learn again that obediently pointing to the Lord in all things (again, glorifying God as the only perfect example for everyone to follow) brings a closer relationship with Him—for us and others. We always give God the glory out of gratitude for what Jesus did to redeem us, and He's our Creator, but a nice side benefit is our increased peace, love, and joy.

We baggage-laden addicts were two of the least likely to bring significant glory to our Lord, but the one constant throughout our entire relationship has been a mutual, relentless pursuit of biblical truth. From facilitating our *Recovery in Christ* study around this time, we were becoming more and more able to recognize the schemes of the enemy and establish victory for Jesus through trust in Scriptures like Revelation 12:11:

> *"They triumphed over him by the blood of the Lamb and by the word of their testimony; they did not love their lives so much as to shrink from death."*

For Mia and me, the enemy's attacks kept coming, but we continually dismissed our defeated foe, something I was quickly learning the importance of. As Christians, we can be our own worst "enemy" when we open doors for the adversary. That is especially true with our uncontrolled mouths, which has been my major struggle: I speak when I should remain silent and vice versa. But this has greatly decreased and will one day go completely away—in this life or the next—as I continue seeking biblical answers. James 3:5-6 gives helpful advice about the dangerous and destructive weapon we possess with the ability to speak. He begins by comparing verbal self-control to boats:

> "Take ships as an example. Although they are so large and are driven by strong winds, they are steered by a very small rudder wherever the pilot wants to go. Likewise, the tongue is a small part of the body, but it makes great boasts. Consider what a great forest is set on fire by a small spark. The tongue also is a fire, a world of evil among the parts of the body. It corrupts the whole body, sets the whole course of one's life on fire, and is itself set on fire by hell. All kinds of animals, birds, reptiles, and sea creatures are being tamed and have been tamed by mankind, but no human being can tame the tongue. It is a restless evil, full of deadly poison."

And you must love the wisdom of Proverbs:

> "Starting a quarrel is like breaching a dam; so drop the matter before a dispute breaks out."
> (Proverbs 17:14)

> "Even fools are thought wise if they keep silent, and discerning if they hold their tongues."
> (Proverbs 17:28)

God has a lot to say about keeping our mouths shut! Disciplining our own speech should help us extend grace to others who mouth off, instead of shooting back our own lethal sparks. As Christians, we learn that the Holy Spirit is the only One who can tame our tongues.

Unfortunately, this is a lesson I'm still learning after fifty-two years of seeking worldly wisdom and finding mostly deceptions—some that nearly put me in an early grave. But now my heart and mind are open to God's wisdom. For years I have been daily studying Proverbs, but even with that epic book of knowledge it will probably take a lifetime to grasp even a glimmer of God's unfathomable understanding; it may be unlikely to learn one percent of His mind, even well into eternity. But no matter how much the Lord might bless me with more biblical wisdom, I strive to be like the Apostle Paul, who humbles himself here in Philippians 3:12–14:

"Not that I have already obtained all this, or have already arrived at my goal, but I press on to take hold of that for which Christ Jesus took hold of me. Brothers and sisters, I do not consider myself yet to have taken hold of it. But one thing I do: Forgetting what is behind and straining toward what is ahead, I press on toward the goal to win the prize for which God has called me heavenward in Christ Jesus."

Getting back to spiritual warfare, attacks from the enemy are real for unbelievers *and* Christians, but Hebrews 4:12 tells us nothing can stand against the power of Scripture:

"For the word of God is alive and active. Sharper than any double-edged sword, it penetrates even to dividing soul and spirit, joints and marrow; it judges the thoughts and attitudes of the heart."

From Genesis 1 to Revelation 22, the double-edged sword of Scripture stops the enemy dead in his tracks; he *cannot* stand against the Lord's Truth. For further study on spiritual warfare, Ephesians 6:10–20 teaches offensive and defensive strategies that guarantee victory over Satan—putting on the full armor of God.

As Mia and I spent time searching the Bible for protection from the enemy's attacks—often mental assaults—we drew nearer to our Heavenly Father, He drew nearer to us, and we drew nearer to each other. Again, the Lord kept leading us straight to the cross. We faced major storms in April when God was stretching my faith through Mia's struggles with the idea of *us* and *our* future—transitioning from just *her*, to *we*. This meant difficult times for me. Bridling my tongue became key.

The Holy Spirit gave me enough discernment to know that Mia may still be on the fence, maybe even wanting to postpone the wedding or possibly walk away entirely. Even after receiving what she knew to be the *third and final* dove confirmation—the one that once and for all convinced her that God meant for us to become one in marriage—for her, the Lord's plans still had a cloud of doubt over them, especially the idea of having a wedding so soon.

But I knew how much time Mia had been spending with our Savior and the amazing relationship that had come from it, so I only needed to remain silent and pray for the Holy Spirit to speak to her heart. Why get in the way of what God was doing? My verbal self-control went better than ever before—which is not saying much—until I decided to allow the Spirit to make amends for me. I asked His guidance in helping me write to the person I love about what was on my heart. Here's the email I sent Mia on April 24th (because of the length I will not italicize):

"Mia, I want you to know...first and foremost...I *love* you so very much and all of this saddens me, no end! I understand where there might be doubts regarding my capabilities as a provider and spiritual leader. Please understand, I am a 52-yearold man who has made bad choices, and by God's grace, mercy, and righteousness has been restored to a healthy, vibrant, and loving man of God. I've said all along that you are a part of the process. I know you are a gift from God to be my helper. Please know, you've never stunted my growth, only encouraged it. And truth be told...you've helped me along at breakneck speed.

"I have no regrets for the way it was, the way it is now, and the way it will be with God being first in our lives. I have *no* fear of the future. I am willing to take advice, make changes, and focus on God's will for me, you, and us. No matter how convicted I am about what I believe, like how you are the one and we should be married on the day of Pentecost as planned...there's a chance my beliefs are misguided. So, I will remain an open vessel and listen for wisdom from above, including when it comes from those who know better than I. We certainly have godly married couples who would gladly lend us some guidance.

"This is only me speaking for me. You have your own walk, so please know...I'm not pushing my will on you by writing this to you. I'm merely letting you know that by His stripes I am healed! Every day I walk with Him...I'm growing...sometimes quickly, sometimes slowly, but it's growth! Furthermore, nothing that has happened in my past has any bearing on our future. It was necessary for me to go through what I did and there are possibly some consequences I may face in the future.

"However, with God's wisdom and the love He has for me and us...I will be grateful for these trials and tribulations as they strengthen my and our faith. I will continue to walk by faith and not by sight. If I do not, what I see in the natural will discourage me: I will stop and give up. I fully believe if I stay in faith and trust in God's promises...I will be delivered from whatever is troubling me and us. Jesus says:

'Come to me all who are weary and burdened, and I will give you rest.' (Matthew 11:28)

"And this is where I will remain...in His rest. I surrender all to Him and I know He is with me. One final thought...I believe I have been doing everything through this rough patch without total *love* in my heart...it's a bit self-righteous on my part to believe I have enough faith for both of us. Shame on me and I'm truly sorry. No matter what happens, I must continue loving you through this with kindness and compassion. After all, this is the true nature of Christ and I need to be more like Him and less like me (the old me) ... Again, I am truly sorry for my past behavior. I. . .*love*. . .*you*. . .and I need to be better at showing you by my actions and not just by my words. . . Amen, Robby"

Not long after I sent that email, while wedding plans were on hold and we waited for God's plans, Mia's "what-if" fears and other unknowns began to subside. Though it would not seem possible during all the relationship strain, God was yoking us even more together, and in ways only He can; going forward we would increasingly be blessed by signs, miracles, and wonders. As we kept leaning into and being more obedient to His Word, our faithfulness and prayers allowed God to reveal more and greater insights, producing positive results, like Mia always believing in us even though she struggled with my financial situation and often ugly, flawed humanness. And we continued being transparent with one another and praying for each other daily, something Jesus's disciple instructs us to do in James 5:16:

"Therefore confess your sins to each other and pray for each other so that you may be healed. The prayer of a righteous person is powerful and effective."

Through James, God tells us we were created to transparently work through our issues *together*, always in communication with Him and each other. Confessing sins and praying for each other releases us from the laws of sin and death. When talking with others, ask the Holy Spirit's guidance for when to speak and when to tame your tongue until a more appropriate time. Be patient, continue communicating, and if it is the Lord's will, He will yoke two people *together* for His glory. Matthew 12:25 tells us what happens when we let strife build because we do not communicate, are not transparent, and don't pray for each other:

> *"Jesus knew their thoughts and said to them, 'Every kingdom divided against itself will be ruined, and every city or household divided against itself will not stand.' "*

At ten months into our relationship, though neither of us would have admitted it, we were both selfish; most people don't realize that blind spot of deception in their own lives. Though Mia and I both probably felt we were in the best spiritual condition of our lives, we were hypocrites. During those many months since we met, the Lord was circumcising our hearts through trials and tribulations involving fear, doubt, and a desire for self-preservation. As you would expect from a loving God, over time He reveals our areas of unrighteousness that need pruning. First John 5:6–9 talks about the testimony that comes from the water and blood (Jesus), along with the Holy Spirit. God was using those three to purge Mia and me from the inside out:

> *"This is the one who came by water and blood—Jesus Christ. He did not come by water only, but by water and blood. And it is the Spirit who testifies, because the Spirit is the truth. For there are three that testify: the Spirit, the water, and the blood; and the three are in agreement. We accept human testimony, but God's testimony is greater because it is the testimony of God, which he has given about his Son."*

During those ten months, God used the water of His Word to continually wash Mia's and my broken—but willing—hearts while covering us with Christ's blood for the forgiveness of our sins. At the same time, His Spirit rapidly revealed the truth of who He created each of us to be. And that last one included how the two of us would become one on June 8th, 2014. Walking with our Savior through all the struggles, we often experienced fun, excitement, gratification, and tears of joy, especially in May because God was further along in yoking our hearts together. We were two people equally on fire to fulfill *His* will and not *our own,* which meant many of "our" wedding plans were still unknown while we waited on Him to reveal what *His* would be. This pause to seek and wait on His final instructions kept us looking for answers where we always should: at the cross.

Contrary to the mayhem most couples go through a month before marriage, we were at peace. May was about not getting ahead of God—just waiting on His guidance. Even though the ceremony was a couple weeks away, we appeared to have no wedding plans! But that would be the world's view of our situation, while the reality was that we were yoked to Christ's kingdom. In John 18:36, Jesus proclaimed:

"My kingdom is not of this world."

That means His followers are no longer of this world. Though we had no plans for "our" wedding, God did, so we only needed to wait a bit longer for His specific instructions. Imagine how much Scripture-induced faith it would take to have that sort of "peace which passes all understanding" in *our*—really, *His*—situation. Instead of last-minute scrambling, we had finally surrendered to our divine wedding Director, allowing Him to orchestrate His plans for our ceremony; there is so much freedom when you let go and let God.

Of course, God wants us to be looking for His solution, so we recognize when He does send a boat to rescue us from the rooftops during a flood. Instead of sitting idle, we continually discussed what we thought our Heavenly Father might be up to with His plans. I think the Lord enjoys that sort of interaction where two of His kids are whole-heartedly seeking His will for their lives.

Along came a boat, a day of revelation—May 18th. I'll never forget that beautiful Sunday afternoon when Mia and I were driving on one of Tampa's main drags. We had our windows rolled down and the sunroof open, while having another conversation about what God might be thinking with the June 8th date and no wedding plan in sight. We were sitting at a red light when Mia suddenly recognized a prophetic pattern: there next to us was a car playing rap music extremely loud.

Mia excitedly recalled the same scenario happening to her just one day before, saying that was *the second time in two days that she had been at the same intersection, sitting next to a car loudly playing rap music. She said both times made her curious as to why people play it so loud.*

Then that deja-vu moment prompted her to recognize God speaking louder than the rap music: Mia suddenly flipped to shouting:

"The license plate! The license plate! Oh my gosh, we have to look at the license plate!"

I immediately recalled the wedding date we had seen on a car's tag when we met the jeweler for coffee. So of course, I wanted to take a look at this loud car's license plate, and I still get chills thinking about God's message:

Calculate the mathematical probabilities of that car showing up with conspicuously loud music that would bring our attention to it, then we recognize it as the one license plate we should look at that day, and it ends up directly answering the question we were just asking God:

"Lord, are You sure You want us to be married on June 8th?"

His answer had our God-connection-number *222*, followed by an *8* for the 8th and *JN* (the official two-letter abbreviation for June). Oh yeah, it just happened to be an "IN GOD WE TRUST" license plate! Add to that the previous car Mia was unusually attracted to the morning we ordered the *wedding* ring: *SO8 222 (222, SO the 8th)*. Over and over the Lord had been declaring how Mia and I are *better 2 gether*—or *better 222 gether*.

So, God was telling us to stay the course with His wedding date, and when I had first visited the St. Augustine cross, He individually confirmed that sacred place as the spot for my proposal to Mia. The ring was in my possession after making the final payment to Blake, and Mia had made Memorial Day arrangements for us to take her boys to St. Augustine. Though I had been around them several times, this would be three days together morning, noon, and night. Neither boy knew I would be proposing to their mother. Fortunately, Mia's father would be there, giving me the chance to ask him for permission to marry his daughter.

That Wednesday evening before the weekend when we would be heading to the cross, Blake and I had our usual time in the Scriptures, after which I made the nightly call to Mia so we could talk and pray before bed. I had been wanting to make the coming proposal special for her, so after hanging up the phone I asked the Lord what she might appreciate. The Holy Spirit's answer came quickly and clearly with a proposal poem I would read to Mia at the cross that Saturday: *222 Says It Was Always You*

Since we're here at the cross it had to be true,
Just look at signs, miracles, and wonders of 222.
When He first showed us, we discerned whether to believe,
Now on this day in May, I'm down on one knee.

Your tiny palm in my hand and tears in my eyes,
Asking if you'll have me all the days of our lives.
I promise to love you, placing your needs before mine,
Honoring the Lord's gift from heaven's most divine.

God knew I loved you before you were born,
My heart now mended from all the years it was torn.
222 says it was always you,
Just ten months, but honey, look at all we've been through.

We've laughed, we've cried, been mad, and still grew,
Agape is our love and Jesus is our glue.
This poem almost over as my knee grows tired,
But there's no end to what God has so faithfully inspired.

A love that will last with Christ at the center,
Without fear or doubt for which no evil can enter.
Only God makes angels with heavenly eyes so blue,
My heart is pounding as I await to hear you say, "I do."

If the answer is yes, let's continue this poem,
As I'll surely be hugging you and kissing you all the way home.
A new journey begins with us closer to becoming one,
Tomorrow brings us joy as we watch the rising sun.

Still, today at this cross was a dream come true,
Knowing full well, 222 said, "It was always you."
Dedicated to Mia...the one I've loved before she was born,
Always and Forever, Robby.

That was penned just after midnight on May 22, 2014. Coincidence? Well, consider that this *222* day was a Thursday, so that evening would be our Bible study where we would be excited to let our pastors know the wedding was definitely on for a few weeks later. They, Blake, Sybil, and a few others from our Bible study family were invited and would play an important part in the ceremony. At this point God was speaking clearly about who would be in attendance and what their purpose was to be. It truly was becoming more of God's plan—and we were listening. When we got to Bible study, Mia noticed I had a different Bible with me than the one I normally carry. I actually gave it to a new-Christian friend who did not have a Bible. Mia knew something I had forgotten about the Bible I brought, so she pointed out the inside cover where she had written "December 29, 2013" and "222," for the date and room number of our first stay together in St. Augustine.

Beginning that evening's study, the pastor asked us to open our Bibles to Acts 2 which is about the day of Pentecost (which would be on June 8th that year, our wedding date). As usual we took turns reading. About thirty minutes in, a group member starting reading Acts 2:22. I began to weep! Sitting next to me and excited from the Acts 2:22 revelation, Mia asked if I was okay. I could barely reply with a yes. Although I am often emotional when reading God's Word, Mia could see the revelation I was experiencing was way more intense than my normal weeping. I was sobbing at this point, having difficulty composing myself. Though Mia wanted me to tell her why I was overly emotional, I would not share it right then because it was not yet time: we were *two* days from the proposal. Of course, Mia recognized the three twos that had shown up in important ways during our relationship, but this new, significant occurrence would be revealed to her with the reading of the 222-proposal poem at the cross that weekend. Here is that verse:

> *"Fellow Israelites, listen to this: Jesus of Nazareth was a man accredited by God to you by **miracles, wonders, and signs,** which God did among you through him, as you yourselves know."*

God vouched for Jesus through supernatural acts that happened around Him, including wonders Christ performed on the Day of Pentecost.

Summing up the 222 messages we seemed to have received from God thus far, on May 22, 2014, I penned Mia's proposal poem about the 222s popping up in our relationship, and now here we were reading Acts 2:22 about signs, miracles, and wonders that God uses to send messages. When that verse was read aloud, instantly all God was doing with Mia and me became clear, which was the reason for my tears. Remember how hotel room 222 in St. Augustine was where we opened the curtains to see *the* cross of this story, *God's* story, centered in the window. Then on the way back to Tampa, Mia's mom let her know that Mia had been born in a room 222, and her late grandfather was born on 2/22. He was a man who also loved the Lord but struggled with the same alcoholism as Mia—a curse that was now broken off from the family bloodline—praise God! When going to get the engagement ring, Mia was drawn to a license plate with that number and our wedding date: SO8 222. Then God answered the question we were just asking Him (about whether our wedding should be on June 8th) by drawing Mia to a loud car with the same message: 222 8JN.

And I haven't even mentioned how another sort of plate was also confirmation. One night while washing dishes that Mia had been using for years, we noticed this brand on the manufacturer's stamp: *"222 Fifth Avenue."*

Also remember how God revealed Matthew 22:2 while I was writing the title for chapter 20: "Our Wedding Plans?" Again, that verse is a parable from Jesus about a *wedding* banquet:

"The kingdom of heaven is like a king who prepared a wedding banquet for his son."

It says a *King* prepared a *wedding* banquet for His *son!*

With the reading of Act 2:22 that night at our Bible study, my logical mind stopped calculating the probability of these "coincidences." I needed no more confirmation that our Heavenly Father was orchestrating kingdom moves with our (His) wedding, a union that would work diligently for Christ. And He also knew we would tell this relationship story, bringing Him much glory—rightly so.

Unfortunately, some will claim these incredible wonders, miracles, and signs were just happenstance; they will not accept hardcore data from two credible witnesses, who even hold physical proof of these instances, like all the pictures presented. They will not believe, even with all the evidence of an intelligent Creator communicating with His creation through His love language of miracles, wonders, and signs. Yet, many of the same look out at the vast expanse of space and are completely convinced there are other forms of intelligent life in the universe, just because people have reported seeing UFOs.

Besides all the above, how about the Holy Spirit using me to pen the poem *Wake Me at Three to See God's Glory* that references the first of four blood moons, the subject of Acts 2:20? That is followed by Acts 2:21, a verse about calling on the name of the Lord to be saved, like I did that Sunday morning at the Salvation Army Chapel. BTW, the picture of my bible with the 222 on the inside corner and the date of December 29, 2013, was the bible I was given as a Salvation Army Beneficiary. Then comes Acts *2:22* mentioning how God communicates through *signs, miracles, and wonders.*

It is clear God had my and Mia's relationship parallel chapter 2 of Acts. In fact, my journey with God started in the *Graham* (my last name) House at the *ACTS* Detox Center—the same place where Mia would be facilitating AA meetings two years later. God created time, and He is the only Being who lives outside of it, so He has seen the future for all of us. That means the Lord knew all along that Mia and I would end up using our story to glorify His name—*and* all along *He* has known that *you* would one day read this book! So don't be surprised when you start experiencing God-incidents for yourself; it's how the kingdom of heaven works when you are open to receiving.

In fact, many of us who have read the Old Testament may have thought how cool it would be to have God speak to us like He did to many in history. But He still does! Even today our Heavenly Father loves speaking to each of His children—that includes me and *you*. But are you listening? To learn *His* plan? *The* plan for you? The Lord desperately wants to reveal Himself to you, and the first step toward that is a commitment by you to study His Word daily. God wants to talk with you. Open your Bible. He's waiting. Our Heavenly Father wants a relationship with every one of His children, so He provides nudges, winks, and prompts to let you know He is listening and speaking back to you. Trust me, you will not regret it!

The miraculous revelation from Thursday night Bible study had me even more focused on the cross of Christ, especially the one where I would propose to Mia that weekend. The next day, we and Mia's boys loaded up the cars and headed for the upper east coast of Florida. Once there we spent some time with Mia's family, and I was able to ask her father to approve of me asking his daughter's hand in marriage. The previous year it might have been *no*. But he agreed—praise God.

Waking Saturday morning, the boys had plans with their grandfather, uncle, and cousin, so we set up a time to meet later in downtown St. Augustine, and then Mia and I headed straight to the cross. Before leaving, I made sure the ring and poem were in my pockets. I could sense Mia knew what was coming but of course she had none of the details. It was an absolutely beautiful day in coastal Florida as we walked the long path to the cross.

Still a good distance away, Mia's mind was blown when God further confirmed His presence with ringing church bells. Mia stopped dead in her tracks, looked at her watch, and told me it was 3:45. This was another of the consecutive-number patterns that she had become very familiar with. Here's the backstory: like Jesus being opposed by Peter before going to the cross, we experienced major opposition before this proposal trek to the St. Augustine cross. The previous day in Tampa, Mia received a challenging phone call from a well-meaning person in our lives. Shaken, she stepped outside from her appointment and called me for prayer. At that moment, nearby church bells rang, and she saw by her watch that it was 3:45. For quite some time, God had been graciously revealing His perfect alignment with her through sequential numbers. Even while stopping to gas up for our trip, the person before her pumped $12.34. Who does that? So, by God's design and no plan of our own, we were walking to the cross with church bells ringing at exactly 3:45—just like those that had rung at the same time the previous day in a different city—confirming perfect alignment with the Lord. These signs brought Mia God's peace.

We saw people sitting in the wooden swing at the foot of it. Mia mentioned how she had really wanted to sit there with me, so she hoped they might decide to leave before we got there—and they immediately got up and walked away. So far, so good. There at the Matanzas River, where it is close to emptying into the Atlantic Ocean, we reached the foot of that colossal, majestic cross. We only sat a few moments before I slid off the swing, dropped to one knee, took Mia's hand, and began to read *222 Says It Was Always You*. We could both sense prophecy being fulfilled at Mia's "I do." Then cannons fired! Boom Boom! Real cannons! Spanish settlers had brought cannons when Ponce de Leon came to the area in search of the legendary fountain of youth. Next to the cross is a small representation of that supposedly rejuvenating well, along with replicas of Spanish cannons.

They are shot off a couple times per day, and this day they fired as Mia was agreeing to marriage and I was sliding the ring on her finger. Our Lord is an epic God who wants to show off for us, so we need to be looking for those moments; then sit back and enjoy the fireworks. Immediately after the poem proposal, acceptance, ring donning, and cannon blasts, Mia got up to take a photo of a large, beautiful monarch butterfly that landed on a nearby flower—maybe as more of God speaking to us through His creation.

The next morning as a newly engaged couple, Mia and I woke early to catch the sunrise over Crescent Beach. We walked across the street to public access point 727, the same place Mia had encountered the "gentleman" who disappeared right after giving her a word of knowledge. As mentioned earlier, we believe he was her angel unaware, something mentioned in Hebrews 13:2:

"Be not forgetful to entertain strangers: for thereby some have entertained angels unawares."

The first time I asked Mia for coffee was July 27th of 2013 (7-27-13), and now here we were almost eleven months later, engaged as we stood at angelic beach entry point 727, which also happens to be the area code for my cellphone. We were there celebrating God's goodness, standing on *Crescent* Beach—a name that represents the phases surrounding a *new* moon—as a *newly* engaged couple.

Speaking of "coincidences" (again, ancient Hebrew had no such word in its language), we know God made the heavens and earth in six days and then sat back on the seventh to rest and admire His magnificent creation. Four thousand years later Jesus would hang on a tree to glorify God by saving you and me. Christ's final words were, "It is finished." Roughly two thousand years later, Mia and I were at that beach on Sunday morning, May 25th. That was seven days after May 18th when He drew our attention to a *second* license plate that instructed us to go ahead with the marriage on June 8th, 2014, the Day of Pentecost.

Since seeing the car tag on that first Sunday, many more events were orchestrated by God, leading up to my proposal at the cross six days later—when His yoking work with the two of us finally came to fruition. Now here on the seventh day since that sure message from our Lord, Mia and I were engaged and basking in His presence as we sat resting and relaxing on "Crescent Beach", rejoicing in God's glorious sunrise and our union He put together. Elated and in awe, we reclined on the beach that seventh day, finally feeling like, "it is finished"—a phrase our Lord also communicated with the embrace of His beautiful, bright morning sun. He had led us straight to the cross. . .where we found peace and rest in Him.

25

"His Wedding Plans"

On Memorial Day, as an engaged couple, we and the boys drove back to Tampa with Mia admiring her beautiful new ring. But being just two weeks from the wedding, we were both consumed with, "What now!?" Mia needed to inform her teenage sons that mom would be getting married—soon. And though I had not been a father before, I would become a stepfather who did not have the foggiest idea of how to navigate those uncharted waters, which made me nervous and excited at the same time. My previously self-centered life kept me from the gift of children, but now God was giving me the chance to be an additional positive role model for these boys who already had an excellent dad, someone I admire and have become close friends with. Oh yeah, the date of December 29, 2013, on the inside of my bible is their dad's birthday. Go figure!

Just a couple weeks from June 8th, God's specific wedding directives were not popping up on license plates, and our previous plans had become faded memories. But the Lord supplied many inexplicable events over the next thirteen days that led to a beautiful, supernatural variation on the fairytale wedding Mia had been looking for. Of course, none of our relationship up to that point had been like a classic fairytale, but then much of myths, fables, and legends are made-up details about somewhat fictitious people, creatures, and lands.

Contrary to an endless parade somewhat-fictitious stories, the Bible gives eyewitness accounts of real people in history, bygone days involving authentic bravery, heroism, cowardice, failure, victory, love, hate, fear, and profound faith, recounted events that all bring glory to our Heavenly Father. Scripture reminds us that what we're given is not for *our* glory, but to point to *God's* goodness, love, and truth. Again, as the only perfect Being in all creation, our Supreme Being is the *One* example we should emulate, point to, and point others toward. That is why we must give *all* glory to God whenever anything positive happens in our lives. We need to do that every day, as Jesus did.

To back this up, I'll ask you to think about these questions: What did Jesus die for? Was it for people? You and me? Mankind? Yes. . .however, Bob Sjogren of *UnveilinGlory.com* explains this about God-glorifying Christianity versus selfish Christianity:

> *"The contention that Jesus died for us is not wrong, it's just incomplete."*

As Jesus is close to experiencing one of the most torturous deaths possible, John 12:28 reveals Him talking to our Heavenly Father, and Christ reveals the main reason He came to earth (followed by the Father showing His pleasure at His Son's statement):

> " *'Father, glorify Your name!' Then a voice came from heaven: 'I have glorified it, and I will glorify it again.' "*

Jesus primarily allowed His own excruciating murder as a way to bring God glory through the redemption of *all* creation, including trees, peas, bees, fleas, donkeys, the planet Mercury, and you and me. So, He did die for us, but "above" anything else, Christ died to glorify the Father.

That truth often brings up a legitimate question from fallen mankind: Is God selfish for wanting all the glory? No, our Lord understands that He made us to worship Him—because, as I've mentioned, our Creator is the only perfect example of truth and love—so pointing to Him is what we were made for; when we do so, we live a more joyful life. Jesus has delayed His return for 2000 years so that more people will have time to give their lives to Him before the wrath of God is poured out in the seven-year Tribulation. Besides redeeming all creation, Christ's mission on our planet was to tell the truth of the Trinity, and that means our Christian assignment is to do the same: always pointing people toward God's goodness, salvation through Jesus, and the companionship possible with an indwelling of the Holy Spirit.

Conversely, if we use our freewill to practice self-centered Christianity, treating God like our personal concierge—after all, Jesus died for *us*, right?—then even as Christians we can live an unhappy life. But if we instead give God glory through all circumstances, the fruits of the Holy Spirit are our reward in this life and after: love, joy, peace, patience, kindness, goodness, faithfulness, gentleness and self-control. That said, do we glorify God for that sort of gain? No, we do so to thank Jesus for all

He did, and that righteous attitude happens to have all those wonderful side benefits.

Getting back to obedience, once you and I trust that God created us each for a unique purpose, we can ask Him to reveal His plan for us, wait for Him to speak, and then follow His instructions. With all our requests, if they align with God's goals for us, He is faithful to fulfill our heart's desires. But be prepared to learn that your yearnings may not be in alignment with God's will for your life. The majority of worldly, human desires are more extravagant than necessary and won't produce the joy we expect. Fortunately, our Creator knows what we need, and He has written those desires on our hearts.

Knowing this, we trusted that God's wedding plans would be better than ours. As surrendered vessels tuned into God, we were seeking His directives, but with the wedding one week away, so far, we had heard only crickets, and we planned to spend most of that day at a high-school graduation reception for my friend's son. Seven days from the big event—a timeframe surely seen as madness by anyone who has planned a wedding—that morning Mia began searching the internet for potential ceremony venues. She located a possibility on St. Pete Beach: The Tradewinds resort, which had a webpage background that matched the shorts I was wearing. So, we decided to go check it out in the late afternoon.

Before leaving for the graduation and reception after, Mia and I grabbed the accumulated pocket change we had been throwing into a glass jar for six months. We headed to a grocery-store coin machine to find out the total of what we'd saved as a small bit of extra help with the wedding expenses. What do you suppose are the odds that those loose coins added up to $222? Well, they didn't. The total was $222.72—close enough. In the natural world this outcome would be virtually impossible, but through that amazing supernatural sign, God was telling us (and now you) to trust what Jesus proclaimed in Mark 10:27:

> *"With man it is impossible, but not with God. For all things are possible with God."*

Over two hundred dollars richer, we traveled forty miles to my friend's house, and the whole way we talked about our lack of wedding plans. Incredibly, neither of us was anxious, though we certainly sat ready to hear from the Lord. Later we had only one venue to see, and it was on St. Pete Beach. We had experienced potential God moments when considering the Clearwater Beach area, but those room prices were outrageous. This made Mia wonder if God wanted us married on St. Pete Beach. We chuckled at our journey that had gone from Blake's house on the river, to Clearwater Beach, and now maybe St. Pete Beach.

On the way to the graduation reception, we looked carefully for more signs—like road signs; yes, that had become one recognized way God spoke to us, and since He knows His kids well, why would our Father not continue using that language. We arrived at the house of my longtime friend Jay. He and his fiancée Stacy would be meeting Mia for the first time, and they were curious about our relationship since they had been dating many years before deciding to get married, while Mia and I were forming that precious union within one year of meeting.

We began to share our testimony, like how the jar of wedding change came to $222. God loves when Christians tell of His wonders because it draws the listeners closer to Him. The more we glorify God by recounting what He has done in our lives and the lives of others, the more He will reward us with more signs, miracles, and wonders. We also shared the Bible passages from Acts, further letting them know how God confirmed and reconfirmed our wedding date. Although my friend Jay was a wonderful guy (the one from earlier in this story who hooked me up with my Mercedes after the death of my pathetic junker) and an outstanding father, he was not a follower of Christ, so he and Stacey probably thought we were crazy—rightfully so. Besides the seeming wackiness of this God-encounter talk, the old Robby he knew had been a drug-addicted, hellraising maniac; now here I was talking about divine, supernatural guidance from God that was leading me to marriage the next weekend. He also knew my ex-wife and how twisted that relationship was, so he had to be thinking I was still some kind of madman. Those seeing through earthly eyes cannot recognize miracles occurring in the lives of surrendered Christ followers.

But it appeared that Stacy knew the Lord, telling Jay that the two of them needed to get back in church. From some of the dreams she had been having, Stacy seemed convicted of her Heavenly Father's involvement in her life. She even had her own God number—217—which she awoke a few times to see on her bedside digital clock. I already had my phone's Bible app open, so I read her Acts 2:17:

> "In the last days, God says, I will pour out my Spirit on all people. Your sons and daughters will prophesy, your young men will see visions, your old men will dream dreams."

Possibly because her children were also experiencing spiritual dreams, Stacy wept as she told Jay that Mia and I had shown up for a higher purpose, and the two of them needed to think about attending church together. My friend Jay was understanding and also seemed somewhat moved by our conversation. Today they are happily married and doing well. We believe God planted seeds that afternoon, and we know He has been faithful to water them, especially since we continued appealing to Him on the matter through prayer and supplication. Driving away later, Mia and I were grateful that God used us *together* for His glory.

Arriving in the parking lot at the Tradewinds, Mia saw an old friend, exchanged small talk, and let me know this person was "one of us," meaning she too struggled with addiction. Her issue had been alcohol and it may have still been so at that time. Because Mia and I had been facilitating a *Recovery in Christ* group and were fifty miles from home, this sort of improbable meeting caused us both to lean into the conversation, paying close attention for however God may want to help the person through us.

Finishing that encounter, Mia and I prayed before entering the resort. Upon entering we first noticed that all around us was hustle and bustle, causing Mia to stop and comment that it didn't feel right. I mentioned how she appeared close to throwing up, and we agreed to leave—but then Mia's feeling changed. She declared herself to be okay and that she thought we needed to press into the place. There at the atrium, we wondered which way to go until Mia suggested we go see the water, so we walked through to a backdoor that opened onto St. Pete Beach.

A bit over an hour before sunset, we slowly wandered a few hundred yards down the beach, ending up at a sister property: the Guy Harvey Outpost resort. There was no one else around where we sat on a lounge chair outside of the pool area. It had rained earlier, so the chairs were a little wet—or maybe "cleansed." After a few minutes, Mia confirmed that the place might work, and that we should find out what the next weekend's rate would be if available.

I found it interesting how I was in the fishing industry at that time, Guy Harvey is an amazing artist who specializes in paintings of sport fishing, and *St. Pete Beach* refers to the Apostle Peter who was a fisherman—and fisher of men—both like me. I immediately felt at home, but the wedding would be about glorifying God and my beautiful wife having the wedding her heart desired, so I let Mia do most of the talking. Derek at the front desk was quite receptive, especially after hearing a bit of our story and giving God the glory for leading us to this hotel. His smile revealed him as a believer, which was confirmed when he mentioned that his real name is

James ("like the Apostle James," he said), but he forgot his name tag that day, so the resort had him wear someone else's. The rate James showed us for a gulf-view suite with a balcony over one of the nicest, soft-white-sand beaches in the world was nothing short of a miracle. We were incredibly impressed with the room, so we gave James positive feedback but let him know we needed to pray for God's direction. As a fellow follower of Christ, James understood and suggested we pray while trying their new restaurant that just opened *that day*.

The massive aquarium we saw when entering the Rumfish restaurant had been featured on the television program *Tanked*—guests could swim in it! Their decor featured a Guy Harvey fishing theme, and the beautiful atrium had big-game fighting chairs with rods and reels; patrons could sit in them and take pictures that looked like they were on a sport-fishing vessel fighting a prize catch. Yes, we had a tourist moment ourselves, as you can see by the next photos.

Miraculously, as Mia had hoped to have in the backyard of Blake's house, the Rumfish featured a menu of *Hawaiian* seafood, fruits, and vegetables. And she immediately noticed the *Hawaiian* flowers used for garnish—in fact, the entire motif of the interior and deck was a Hawaiian luau! The menu showed everything Mia had planned to order from a caterer, praise God!

As sunset approached while eating, and knowing we wanted to be married around that time, we asked the waitress if it would be possible to cover our plates and walk down to the beach. Once we explained why, she was more than happy to oblige. We found a nice area to watch the sun go down and then started back toward the restaurant, hoping to get more confirmation about whether this place was in the Lord's wedding plans. Rounding the corner back through the atrium entrance, Mia abruptly halted, grabbed my arm, and yelled:

"Stop! Look down! This is the place we are to be married!"

We were standing on a large nautical compass. Both of us became covered in chills as Mia told me about a photo, she had pinned to her vision board at the house.

This first picture (next below) was taken on a cruise ship two months before she and I met. Mia was standing on a nautical compass just like the one seen below that was taken this day at the Rumfish. On Mia's cruise, the Holy Spirit had prompted her to back up and take a picture of the floor. Not realizing she was standing on a nautical compass; she took the picture and then felt the Spirit say:

"If you stay the course with me, I'll guide your steps."

Mia's thought was a resounding:

"Fair enough!! I've done it my way for far too long!"

You can see from the two photos that she was wearing the exact same toenail polish, even though Mia switches nail colors like most people change socks. And you may remember the same shade of blue on the wings of that little white dove Mia discovered in her jewelry box. Back then Mia knew the wing color meant something and God would reveal it one day; that significance is shown on her toes with the same color ending up in these pictures. And the dove is a direct reference to the Holy Spirit, Who is referred to as *the Helper* in many Bible translations. Robby and I knew He was helping lead us into His truth and righteousness. Through both of us staying the course with Him, Mia and I landed on the exact spot at the Rumfish, which would testify beyond a shadow of doubt that God was in control of our destiny.

Also, the sandals in the cruise photo featured a prominent *G* that Mia liked to think of as representing *God*, to which I jokingly replied that it could also have been God foretelling her future fiancé, Robby *Graham*. Actually, they were shoes made by *Guess*, which is Mia's mom's maiden name.

There's more: May 24th, 2013, was when she stepped on the cruise ship's compass and God declared that He would guide her steps as long as she stayed the course with Him. That was precisely one year prior to her path leading to our engagement at the cross on May 24th, 2014. Also of note was our arrival date on that trip to St. Augustine: May 23rd was the 143rd day of the year, leaving exactly 222 days remaining in 2014. We hadn't realized some of these "coincidences" until writing this book, but we are faithful to share them as examples of God's strategies used in His divine guidance.

Standing on her second maritime dial at Rumfish restaurant (with same blue nail color she had on when taking a photo of the cruise compass), Mia instantly knew this was the place. So of course, we decided to book it—for the following weekend—but how in the world was it even available? Well, through God's timing, the restaurant just opened that day, so availability was as good as it was ever going to be. Some may still believe we were only finding justification for the wedding date from an overly intense search for signs, but hopefully the impossible odds of all this unfolding together have convinced you of divine destiny: we set sail for St. Pete Beach and then arrived at the Tradewinds that blew us a few hundred yards down the beach to Guy Harvey's Outpost resort. There the Lord confirmed that we were right on course by putting the nautical compass underfoot.

God's continued guidance that we have been reporting though this entire book is a testament to Proverbs 3:5–6:

> *"Trust in the Lord with all your heart and lean not on your own understanding; in all your ways submit to him, and he will make your paths straight."*

The Holy Spirit took us off course from *our* wedding plans and helped us sail to *His*.

Over the next few days, the Lord helped Mia easily reserve the restaurant, find a beautiful cupcake arrangement for the cake, contact friends and family who God revealed as those He wanted at His wedding, coordinate with Sybil about what the two of them would wear, and arrange for Blake and me to have matching outfits that resembled Tom Selleck's Hawaiian wardrobe on his *Magnum P. I.* television show. Mia had already purchased her dress in St. Augustine the day *before* I proposed, "coincidentally" at a small boutique directly across the street from motel room 222, where our curtains opened to the beautiful cross we would journey to—literally and figuratively.

That entire week leading up to the Day of Pentecost on June 8th, the wedding preparations were filled with more undeniable signs from the Lord, like when Mia was at the gym on StairMaster equipment. Her session was about to time out and she wanted to stop, but then felt like the Holy Spirit was having her press on a bit. Less than two minutes later, a woman put down a gym bag next to Mia and got on the machine by her—it was a Guy Harvey bag. Right after, while exiting the gym, she noticed that same black Audi from the night we met the jeweler, the one she admired with license plate *SO8 222*. It was parked right next to her SUV! Any remaining doubt Mia had up to that point was quickly being dealt with in God's supernatural way, so it seemed that all Mia was accomplishing for our special day on St. Pete Beach was directly in alignment with *His* wedding plans.

Not coincidentally (because this too was done by God), we received a surprise call from my brother Mac and sister-in-law Elsie in Michigan, who informed us that they would be starting a Florida vacation—*in a few days*. Since we had just solidified the Lord's wedding plans, they had no idea I was getting married. Of course, we added them to the invitation list of very close friends. The last time I saw Mac was during my deep pain and the resulting pill addiction, so he would see an awesome testimony from my new life of purpose and meaning, a totally transformed man. He would see me living a vibrant life with wonderful godly friends, and how I am in love with a spiritual-warrior, Jesus-loving woman who the Lord chose for me. Mac would learn that all this happened from Christ coming into my life.

Mia told her boys about the wedding, brought them to the beautiful hotel, and the three settled in for the weekend. I'm sure her sons were quite concerned for their mom but were also incredibly supportive. Though it may not have been what they were feeling on the inside, outwardly the two teens were polite and appeared calm. Looking back, the way they handled it was just one more reason I am proud to be their stepfather. The boys are two gifts God gave their mother and then me.

On Saturday I visited them at the resort to help prepare for our Sunday wedding. We prayed together on the beach while basking in the sun, both at peace from God's wedding plans having fallen into place. That day we were able to share the love of Jesus with others around the hotel, something Mia and I were created to do. My and Mia's commitment to the Lord was that we would share the gospel *together* whenever He asked. Actually, witnessing is every Christian's mission until Christ returns, yet some studies estimate 95% of believers never bring another soul to Jesus. God wants more than just you and me to choose heaven, so we all must plant Jesus seeds in those the Lord brings across our paths, and then let the Holy Spirit work on their unbelieving spirits.

I left Mia at the hotel and would not see her until the next day's final setup before our evening wedding. When I stopped by her house to take care of the dogs—beautiful Labrador retrievers, one chocolate and the other yellow—the feeling was strange to think that *her* home and dogs would soon be *ours*. After the wedding, the dogs and I quickly became attached. It seems no coincidence that the *dog*, an animal widely known as man's best friend, is the backward spelling of *God*.

As it got late that night, I knew the Lord had something for me to share with Mia at the wedding, so I asked Him to let me know and then fell asleep. The next morning, I awoke to some quiet devotional time. God's presence was strong all around and I suddenly had my instructions, so I sat at the computer and began to type. The Holy Spirit was giving me a final poem to sum up my and Mia's relationship, and then put the final exclamation point on the Lord's wedding story, which would end this Day of Pentecost. The divine revelation I received had me incorporate each previous poem that the Spirit and I wrote for Mia, even using their titles in the order given during our journey. We will get to it in a minute.

After arriving at the beach, best-man Blake and maid-of-honor Sybil—who both stood by us for the entire journey—helped prepare the beach spot where we would soon marry, laying down an array of decorations like a heart shaped from oyster shells to stand inside and two large, beautiful tiki torches, one for each side of us. During the wedding dry run the day before, Mia had planted one of the torches in the sand to see how hard it would be. Alarmingly, when she turned and bent over to move some shells, a strong gust blew the torch over, right at her! Luckily the large pole grazed my arm, slowing it before the heavy wood struck Mia with a fair blow to the head. She chuckled and then so did I, each of us acknowledging that the enemy had made an attempt, but he had no business near God's wedding. The devil had already lost when Mia and I separately said yes to Jesus.

With the setup complete, guests were arriving as an amazing Florida sunset was developing over the water. As the wedding party took their positions and as I looked up toward the hotel, my gorgeous bride was being escorted by her two boys. Once they got to us, each gave their mother a kiss before releasing Mia to stand next to me. After covering us with the Jewish Tallit (prayer shawl) that Blake and Sybil brought back from Israel, our pastor did an excellent job reading the vows.

Then it was Mia's and my turn to exchange personal messages, which began when Mia surprised me with a poem the Holy Spirit instructed her write, a new version of the second poem I wrote her: "What Is Love?" Here is hers with the underlined words she added or changed from my original poem. God was speaking to her with answers to the poem's question—in a way only He can:

What Is Love?

Oh those days we sit and ponder the question. . . What is love?
Well. . .the answer is divine. . .sent from heaven above.
*Look at **our hearts** once made of stone,*
no longer beating lost and all alone!

*We just lift **our** eyes to heaven and open **our** soul,*
Feel the glory of God when His love begins to flow.
Feel the peace and serenity as the turbulent sea calms,
Like the warmth of a sunset seen through the leaves of palms.

Now, as the day becomes night. . .do not worry,
For His love still shines bright and will never scurry.
Look at the stars so far away,
Beautiful, majestic, and in the heavens they will stay.

Ah. . . What is love? Need you ask more?
*It's right in front of **us**. . .**we've opened** the door.*
***We walked** through, humbled and without fear,*
***Feeling** the Holy Spirit with a smile and a tear.*

You've been touched by love, holy and clean,
My God, my Savior. . . His wonders yet to be seen.
For me it's an angel with wings of gold,
*One with eyes of **hazel** and a spirit that is bold.*

Two become one in the eyes of the Lord,
We're better together with the Bible as our sword.
The enemy has no chance in our house of bricks,
We've both been lost and know all of his tricks.

Destined to save lives in the name of Christ,
We know we're different, blessed, and convicted. . .never
thinking twice!
***We** no longer question. . . What is love?*
We found someone to walk with. . .sent from heaven above.

***Our hearts** no longer empty and hard as that stone,*
*Full of the Holy Spirit and **we're** no longer alone.*

Dropping to our knees each night before bed,
To give thanks and praise before we lay down our heads.

Drifting off to sleep now together as one,
Hearts and souls mended by Jesus, God's Son.
So let's stop questioning. . . What is love?
Just lift your eyes to heaven above.

I wept as Mia read that beautifully written addition to the poem God penned through my hand ten months earlier; she even used props the Lord had given her during our journey, like the blue winged dove Valerie handed her and the stone heart Mia found shortly after I wrote that poem about my heart of stone being changed. With swollen eyes and tears of joy streaming down my face, it was extremely hard to read mine to her. However, garbled it may have come out at the time, here is the poem our Lord instructed me to write and dedicate to my new wife—Mia Revello-Graham—on that special day when we fulfilled *His* wedding plans:

A Gift from Heaven's Most Divine

I knew from the beginning...and God knew before time,
He prepared me "A Gift from Heaven's Most Divine."
From our beginning, He showed us "When Love Is Just Right!"
*That **together**, we'd join Him to walk by faith and not by sight.*

He then revealed to us the meaning of "What Is Love?"
As He gave me you, Mia. . .a gift from heaven above.
Quickly and without haste, our journey had soon begun,
Odds stacked against us, for which each of us could have run.

There was even a time we questioned, "Where Are We Now?"
But with faith in Christ and each other, we managed
somehow.
There was a time we even wondered when two become one,
God's perfect timing showed us to walk with Him and stop
trying to run.

Being obedient to God's word as it was spoken,
We were truly blessed by a love never to be broken.

Revelations came fast and furious, much to our surprise,
We began to know things, hear things, and see with our
spiritual eyes.

You told me of four blood moons and their subsequent story,
Then God inspired me to write "Wake Me at Three to See
God's Glory."
We were now living out chapter 2 in the great book of Acts,
God's words, not ours, for these are just the facts.

So many signs, miracles, and wonders Jesus showed us and
we knew,
That day at the Cross "222 Says It Was Always You."
Fast forward a week to this beautiful evening in June,
We're standing here at sunset, just west of a small dune.

Proclaiming our love for each other as I ask you to be my wife,
With Christ at the center we will have a beautiful life.
So, on this Day of Pentecost, with my angel's hand in mine,
There was never a doubt you were "A Gift from Heaven's
Most Divine."

Our marriage was now official, we kissed, and then we all headed for the restaurant, including my new stepsons, our church family, my brother Mac, and sister-in-law Elsie. Though the list of invitees was scaled down because of the unsettled plans only two weeks prior to the wedding, the Rumfish food (certainly not fish food) was just as Mia had envisioned, and after dinner we exchanged the amazingly tasty cupcakes she requested from a special bakery. Just as God intended, the reception was peaceful and relaxed.

It's interesting to add that God even soothed my financial concerns about racking up debt with the wedding: when we opened the wedding presents during the reception, they were mostly money that ended up covering the cost of us getting married—and then some.

In a while we said the goodbyes and *our* 16-year-old drove his brother to their father's house. There we were alone in our room as husband and wife, living out what was written *eleven*—my favorite number—months earlier in the first two poems God wrote to Mia through my hand. Since we had just begun dating when I started writing them, Mia believes the Lord gave me a gift of prophetic poetry. It's interesting to look at how the Holy Spirit ended those two poems way back then. Here are the last two lines of the first one and final six lines of the second:

Giving thanks and praise to You, Lord, each time I've kissed her good night,
as this gives conviction to "When Love Is Just Right!"

Dropping to our knees each night before bed,
to give thanks and praise before we lay down our heads.
Drifting off to sleep now together as one,
hearts and souls mended by Jesus, God's Son.
So, let's stop questioning. . . What is love?
Just lift your eyes to heaven above.

Now we were newlyweds getting ready for bed, which some may view as coincidence, while others see prophecy fulfilled. Either way, *our* wedding plans were nice, but nothing compared to *His*.

26

"222 *Said* It Was Always You"

We might have ended this story with *His* Day of Pentecost wedding, but of course God continues speaking to us, and one significant example happened almost three years later on May 23rd, 2017. Mia was in our home office on a conference call for Christian Life Coaching. Suddenly the Holy Spirit told her to "flip the calendar," so she glanced at our obviously unused desk calendar and realized it still showed January of 2017. When she flipped forward to May 23rd, the calendar let her know it was the 143rd day of 2017, meaning 222 days were left in the year. Then the Spirit clearly impressed it on Mia's heart that we must finish this book by January 1st of 2018.

Now fast forward to us finishing it exactly 222 days later on December 31st, 2017. It's 11am as I (Robby) am writing, so here we are again at hour 11—and the figurative "11th hour" as far as finishing the Holy Spirit's assignment to complete this book by the end of 2017. Again, all along my and Mia's journey with the Lord, His guidance has really seemed to shine at the last hour, so this made perfect sense for me to be finishing 222 days later at "the last hour." This last-minute writing would be the perfect time for Him to get me a message through my daily Bible study earlier that morning. The Lord chose to wrap this story up by telling you and me who Mia has been since before I met her, continues to be today, and will be for eternity: a wife of noble character. Straight from Proverbs 31:10–31, here's the gift God gave me, my Mia:

> *"A wife of noble character who can find? She is worth far more than rubies. Her husband has full confidence in her and*

lacks nothing of value. She brings him good, not harm, all the days of her life. She selects wool and flax and works with eager hands. She is like the merchant ships, bringing her food from afar. She gets up while it is still night; she provides food for her family and portions for her female servants. She considers a field and buys it; out of her earnings she plants a vineyard. She sets about her work vigorously; her arms are strong for her tasks. She sees that her trading is profitable, and her lamp does not go out at night.

"In her hand she holds the distaff and grasps the spindle with her fingers. She opens her arms to the poor and extends her hands to the needy. When it snows, she has no fear for her household; for all of them are clothed in scarlet. She makes coverings for her bed; she is clothed in fine linen and purple. Her husband is respected at the city gate, where he takes his seat among the elders of the land.

*"She makes linen garments and sells them and supplies the merchants with sashes. She is clothed with strength and dignity; she can laugh at the days to come. She speaks with wisdom, and faithful instruction is on her tongue. She watches over the affairs of her household and does not eat the bread of idleness. Her children arise and call her blessed; **her husband also, and he praises her:** 'Many women do noble things, but you [my Mia] surpass them all.' Charm is deceptive, and beauty is fleeting; but **a woman who fears the** Lord **is to be praised.** Honor her for all that her hands have done, and let her works bring her praise at the city gate."*

That morning the Lord spoke, and I listened, as He talked about having found a wife for me of noble character, and then helped me hold onto her despite my extensive faults. God had Mia and me meet in the least likely of places, one where hopelessness abounds and continues to this day for many—but not for me—praise God! The Lord steadily restored my hope through a gradual understanding of how Jesus Christ miraculously redeemed and transformed this sinful, homeless, penniless, drug addict.

Just as the 66th book completes the Bible, our story finishes with God giving me Psalm 66. Why wouldn't God use a *psalm* (*song*) for my second Scripture reading of the morning. It's about the Jewish exodus out of Egyptian slavery and all they endured on their way to freedom. It wasn't an easy road, but the Lord guided their steps and protected them the whole way. Now here I was in disbelief at how appropriate the passage was that the Lord gave to me on this 222nd day of our assignment to finish the book. I again listened to God speak to me, this time through Psalm 66:1– 12 and 16–20:

> "Shout for joy to God, all the earth! Sing the glory of his name; make his praise glorious. Say to God, 'How awesome are your deeds! So great is your power that your enemies cringe before you. All the earth bows down to you; they sing praise to you, they sing the praises of your name.'

> "Come and see what God has done, his awesome deeds for mankind! He turned the sea into dry land, they passed through the waters on foot—come, let us rejoice in him. He rules forever by his power, his eyes watch the nations—let not the rebellious rise up against him. Praise our God, all peoples, let the sound of his praise be heard; he has preserved our lives and kept our feet from slipping. For you, God, tested us; you refined us like silver. You brought us into prison and laid burdens on our backs. You let people ride over our heads; we went through fire and water, but you brought us to a place of abundance.

> "Come and hear, all you who fear God; let me tell you what he has done for me. I cried out to him with my mouth; his praise was on my tongue. If I had cherished sin in my heart, the Lord would not have listened; but God has surely listened and has heard my prayer. Praise be to God, who has not rejected my prayer or withheld his love from me!"

At the risk of sounding like an infomercial—"But wait, there's more"—I'll also mention how my return to the seafood industry involved dealing with expiration dates on the products we sold. One day while thinking about those sorts of numbers, I was prompted by the Holy Spirit to reflect back on my and Mia's first kiss. It was the day before I attended the Salvation Army's Lake Junaluska Bible conference, which was August 10, 2013, the 222nd day of that year! We did not discover that one until two years into our marriage. It really makes sense when we compare our revelations to what Scripture tells us. Proverbs 25:2 talks about how God enjoys slowly revealing His plan to us as we search for it:

"It is the glory of God to conceal a matter; to search out a matter is the glory of kings."

Do you see how the Lord continually shows us His divine sovereignty? Also testifying to God's divine signs during our journey, my and Mia's code to tell each other "I love you" is 143 (the letter *I* is the number 1, *love* has 4 letters, and *you* has 3). Here's another revelation: when we subtract 143 from 365 days in one year, we get *222*. Just coincidence? Not in this story. God speaks. We must listen. We also discovered that it was the 143rd day of 2013 when Mia was getting ready to set sail on her cruise. There she stood on the nautical compass, being instructed by the Holy Spirit to stay the course because He would guide her steps. And again, just a couple months later, she and her husband to be (me) had their first kiss on the 222nd day of that year.

And here's the exclamation point God provided to tell us that 222 *said* it was always you. Mia often searches for explanations of current events among voices of truth within the body of Christ. One day she read this social media post from 2015 with one man's belief (we know nothing about the author) that those who see a lot of 222s and 2222s in their lives have *it*, which is *the key of King David*:

> *"OK so the 2's have it. So many of you have apparently been seeing a lot of 222 and 2222. . .and are wondering. . .what the Lord might be saying there. Three scriptures that I get for this are Ephesians 2:22, Revelation 22:2 and Acts 2:22.*
>
> *"Ephesians 2:22 is about us being built into a dwelling place for God. Rev. 22:2 is about being trees of life that bring healing to the nations. Acts 2:22 is about being a person of signs, wonders and miracles. All three go together and [when] you see the 222, you are being reminded that you are one [who] is to carry the power and presence of God everywhere you go. A life of the supernatural is yours to step into as you host Him.*
>
> *"Seeing 2222 at key times is about Isaiah 22:22. This is the passage about being given the key of David to open [what] no man can close, and [close what] no man can open. It is about being given a new level of kingdom authority. . . The 2's are all about empowerment, authority, agreement and the supernatural."*[5]

5 https://www.gotquestions.org/born-sinners.html

He is proposing that those who frequently see 222s and 2222s have the key mentioned in Isaiah 22:22:

"I will place on his shoulder the key to the house of David; what he opens no one can shut, and what he shuts no one can open."

Again, Mia and I are *not* numerologists and want nothing to do with the occult numerology of New Age spirituality. That said, God's creation was built on a foundation of His universal math, so it makes sense that He would speak to Mia and me through one particular number. Not giving that passage from Isaiah much more thought, the next couple years Mia and I continued our walk with Christ and managed to receive degrees in Christian counseling from Life Christian University. Since then, we have each added a year of theology. All this biblical study has helped us fall even deeper in love with Jesus and the entire counsel of God's Scripture.

It wasn't until July 4th of 2016 that we learned Isaiah 22:22's significance in our story. For my birthday, Mia had purchased us a Bridal Glory Cruise to the Bahamas. Because my passport had expired, she needed to renew it with my birth certificate, which was included in the trip paperwork she presented me in a box tied shut with a large bow. We were amazed to notice that my birth certificate number is 22225. Seeing is believing!

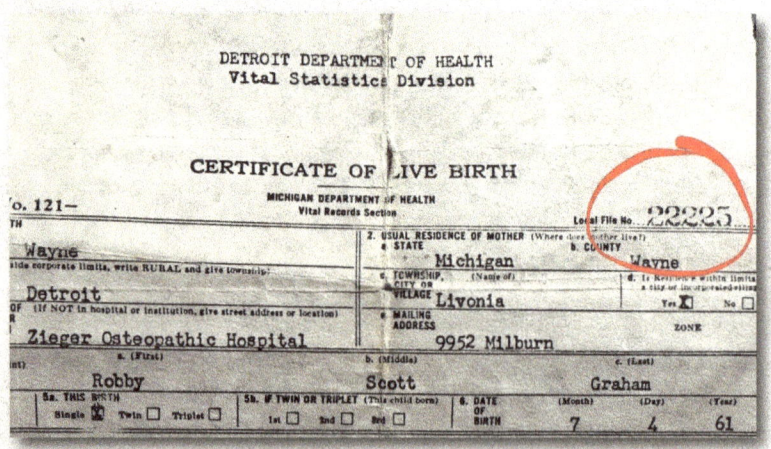

Coincidence? On my 55th birthday we learned that—55 years earlier—the Lord had stamped me with "22225." Did it have to do with Isaiah 22:22? The key of David? And all the 2s? I say, yes.

God gets all the glory for our journey, and as a quick recap:

On April 15th of 2013 I stood looking in the mirror, high on opiates, hating myself, and welcoming death.

Saved in more ways than one on April 28, 2013, I dedicated my life to Christ.

God pointed out Mia as the one for me on July 26, 2013.

Together we endured eleven months of trials and tribulations on our path into alignment with the Lord's plan for our relationship.

He revealed how we are *better together* by communicating in ways we would understand, like presenting us messages attached to the number 222: my birth certificate number is mostly 2s, Mia and I were led to stay in motel room 222 with a perfect view of the St. Augustine cross, it turned out Mia was born in a room 222, our first kiss was on the 222nd day of the year, God drew our attention to 2 license plates with 222 and His desired wedding date, He brought us back to the cross when I proposed with the poem He gave me called *222 Says It Was Always You*, and exactly 2 weeks later we were married.

The Lord communicates with His followers, and even more so when we walk closely with Him, taking to heart what is declared in Proverbs 3:5–6 (a prominent life verse that guides Mia and me):

> *"Trust in the Lord with all your heart and lean not on your own understanding; in all your ways submit to him, and he will make your paths straight."*

Though some will remain skeptics, Mia and I know many of God's chosen will recognize the events in this book as true signs, miracles, and wonders—divinely orchestrated by the Father, Son, and Holy Spirit. Our sovereign Lord will speak to every one of us if we choose to look for, hear, and see what He declares and does.

For those reading who may be hearing Christ's gospel message for the first time, we hope our testimony has opened your heart and mind to the truth of mankind's Savior. Though Mia and I probably do not know your name, God does. Think about how you live on a planet with almost eight billion others, yet how many have your exact DNA or fingerprints? And how many who have ever lived have your DNA or fingerprints? How about all the future people who will ever live: how many will likely have your DNA or fingerprints? The answers are none, none, and none.

That is how detailed and specific God made you. He took great care to make you one of a kind.

And now He enjoys helping you make it through this life—His completely unique creation.

Every moment of every day He is waiting for you to use your free will to choose Jesus as your Savior; that way, the Lord can spend eternity with the one He took such care to distinctively make: you!

For non-believers and Christ followers alike, we should all seek to learn the individual purpose God gave each of us at *conception!* The Lord created you with a personal mission, so He hopes you will not dismiss the miracles, signs, and wonders that He has done and will do to get your attention. In discovering and being obedient to the specific purpose your Heavenly Father created you for, He wants you to more frequently see with your spiritual eyes and hear more clearly with your spiritual ears, turning eventual victory over all life's tests, messes, trials, and tribulations into testimonies about His glory. As Mia's and mine has become, God would have your earthly existence—a short time relative to eternity—turn into a testimony about His goodness, mercy, truth, and love.

Mia and I are examples of chaos and shambles that the Lord redeemed and transformed to tell His message (praise God!). Now that we have been closely bonded to each other through Jesus at the core of our relationship, I hope you can see how God has been using 222 and other signs, miracles, and wonders to tell me and Mia that we will always be together—how we are better together—and always will be.

27

Revelations Café and the Film (2019–2022)

Fast-forward to 2019: Instead of leaving our story at how we lived happily ever after—though we did and still are—five years later our truly close walk with God just got better and better. The blessings *never* ended, and that included using the Christian-counseling degrees and life coaching certifications Mia and I earned. God led us to specific plans for that education, including how Mia set up a life-coaching business. Her logo has a nautical compass with a cross at its center. Pursuing that vocation was God's next step for us, and we were prepared for Him to start sending us clients. We thought He wanted us to coach others about seeking His direction by learning to better hear his voice and see His personal messages. But the Lord did not knock down our door with clients, at least the way *we* expected He would; God's plans for us were so much more amazing than we could possibly imagine!

Of course, Mia continued as a full-time mom, and I kept grinding it out in the seafood industry. Our relationship with the Lord and each other was flourishing, and family times were awesome because God blessed me with *two* amazing stepsons; I was witnessing them grow into fine, godly young men. We enjoyed attending church together as a family, including with the boys' father Martin. Mia was regularly in touch with our Christian life-coach Cynda Harris of Grow Life Coaching Academy (*GrowAndFlourish. com*). Cynda drew revelation out of Mia every time they spoke.

What happened next was more monumental than either of us could have imagined: Mia had been telling Cynda about how Mia's devotional time with the Lord was giving her specific and powerful revelations—downloads from God. She told Cynda about an amazing café, and Mia already knew the name, design, colors, and purpose. She went on to tell Cynda how people would come into this café and sit in the presence of the Holy Spirit, being healed of sicknesses, delivered from depression, set free from addictions, or just enjoying the peace of Christ while being served healthy, plant-based, vegetarian cuisine.

Mia told her how the atmosphere would be filled with the fruits of the Spirit: love, joy, peace, patience, kindness, goodness, faithfulness, gentleness, and self-control. Mia knew there would be a prayer room and wall where people could ask God whatever was on their heart. Once finished laying out the Lord's vision, Mia told Cynda that she just knew God was going to send her a client who might use and fulfill the idea, confirming these truths in an answer to her prayers and the fulfillment of this vision God had given her. Cynda listened intently (as *excellent* coaches like her do), after which she asked Mia the million-dollar question:

"What would make you think this vision is for someone else?"

Mia was stunned, replying, *"Wow! Okay, I'll pray about it."*

From that process, today's Revelations Café was birthed, our amazing witnessing platform that God has given us to have a far-reaching effect on plant- and faith-based communities. We boldly move forward every day in our love for Jesus and the desire to honor the health of our bodies, as temples that house the Holy Spirit. Through a life lived with the Lord, proper nutrition, and regular exercise, we've learned the importance of spirit, mind, *and* body. Today, we have many opportunities to use those degrees and certifications, not only with customers, but also with employees and even online and on-air audiences—many, many God-given interviews and media appearances.

Again, it gets better! Our faulty, human imaginations would not have dreamt it—especially in those days when we had separately hit rock bottom and stared at people of wretched depravity looking back at us in the mirror—but just before we opened Revelations Café (and then again during the Covid scare), a long-lost friend from high school reconnected with me. "Coincidentally," this old friend, John Corry, had already produced two *major* plant-based documentaries that you may have heard of: *Forks Over Knives* and *PlantPure Nation*. He was also just finishing the marketing production of a faith-based documentary about the late football coach and legend Bobby Bowden from Florida State University (FSU). That popular documentary is *The Bowden Dynasty*.

As the Lord would have it, and while we were adding some of the last content to this book, we and John Corry finished filming and released

Revelations Café: Food for the Soul. It continues our true testament to the amazing guidance we have been given by our glorious God and Savior since 2013. The documentary details the continuation of God's epic tale about His redemption and endless love for two of His formerly lost children. The movie relates more aspects of our faith journey, including today's successful restaurant, frozen-meal plans, and our ongoing faith and food events.

Only God knows where we go from here. Possibly, multiple Revelations Café locations? Maybe our and God's story will become a major motion picture? Our imaginations have certainly been stretched over the past few years! Whatever our Lord and Savior wants, we will *always* submit, just as the prophet Isaiah did in this paraphrase and pluralization of Isaiah 6:8 (and by the way, 6/8 was our wedding date, giving us one more confirmation of who we are in Christ):

> *"Then **we** heard the voice of the Lord saying, 'Whom shall I send? And who will go for us?' And **we** said, 'Here **we** are. Send '**us**!' "*

That verse is a confession to God that we both made prior to knowing each other, and now that we're together as one, God knows we are ready for *whatever* comes next. Even when what He gives us seems impossible at first, we chose to obey and walk toward it by faith, because Jesus clearly declared this truth into our hearts through Matthew 19:26:

> *"With man this is impossible, but with God all things are possible."*

Please pray that you, we, and all God's people become and remain *forever* faithful at seeking His will. We pledge to continue proclaiming the goodness of our Lord—Who provided a way out of sin and into an eternity spent in personal relationship with *the Creator of the universe!* As the back of our business cards say (the same declaration Mia's grandfather had on his):

> *"Put God in the Center and Everything Will Fall into Place!"* Amen!!

Introduction to Addendums

What follows are *two* addendums we touched on in our story. How appropriate that the Lord would single out *two* topics to expand on. The first covers the dangers of New Age spirituality, with Mia recounting her experiences in that satanically inspired movement.

The second covers end-times Bible prophecy, something near and dear to both Mia and me (like the rest of Scripture), and so important to understand these days. It's not being preached in the vast majority of Christian churches today, even though it is a huge portion of the Bible and worldwide events, and situations are perfectly lining up with what Scripture tells us is *soon* coming. We all must understand that time is short: Bible prophecy proves that the return of our Lord and Savior is imminent—prompting us to get busy helping Christ's kingdom. This information is not intended to cause fear; it's more for awareness so that we can all help others with what is coming soon.

We hope and pray these brief teachings will strengthen and edify your walk with God.

Addendum 1
New Age

We know that God gives all of us gifts that are meant to help His kingdom, but He also allows us the free will to use them for good, evil, or nothing. I have always felt that uniqueness, and one of my God-given abilities seems to be sensing future events, the sort of spiritual experience church people rarely talk about. But prophesying is widely accepted in the pagan New Age occult movement, a false *religion* I unfortunately gravitated toward much of my life.

God created us to commune with Him and be an active part of His family, so we all have some level of wanting to connect into groups. Until we establish a relationship with the Lord, learn our true purpose, and carry it out, we tend to join worldly teams and end up pursuing what they claim we should be. We work at fitting into something we were never intended for, leading us down a wrong path that keeps us from the joy of the Lord, a problem exponentially worse for me because I *felt* misunderstood or unaccepted.

From my teens I was drawn to the supernatural, and New Age spiritualism is all about that. Our Heavenly Father is a miraculously supernatural Supreme Spirit; while spirits like Satan, demons, and the Antichrist spirit get humans to follow them by performing magic tricks involving healings, signs, and wonders. The deceiver presents himself as an angel of light, easily seducing mankind—including Christians—with his magical, counterfeit miracles.

This duping of believers happens because Christian teachers neglect to educate Christ followers on the spiritual gifts. I did not grow up hearing about Bible *prophecy,* today's sorely neglected quarter to third of the Bible that many Christian churches used to teach over one hundred years ago. My Christian education did not teach much about God's *prophets*, which the pagans called *seers* before the Lord sent some of His own, calling them *prophets*. I was also taught nothing of the prophetic gifts that come with being the Lord's child, so I did not relate my many supernatural experiences with the Bible and how these abilities were to be used for God's kingdom. And Christians learn little about the supernatural Holy Spirit living inside us, the supplier of spiritual gifts.

Among others, some gifts God gave me are words of knowledge (hearing directly from God), glimpses of the future (visions), and a discerning of spirits (in my case, the crazy ability to recognize people with a particularly depraved spirit—by smell!). But before finally seeking God's guidance with my gifts, I naively used New Age (westernized Hinduism) methods involving ungodly spirit guides and other pagan practices like crystals, tarot cards, yoga, reiki, meditation, and many related forms of dark spiritualism. Hindu gurus assure us westerners that *yoga* and *meditation* are *always religious* exercises. These methods—given to them by their millions of gods (spirits)—are for clearing a participant's mind so he or she can more easily become *yoked* with a spirit guide (possessed). Praise God that Christians have the Holy Spirit inside, so He will not allow possession of believers; still, yoga and meditation remain Hindu *religious* practices. Christians meditate on God and His Word, rather than emptying their minds to connect with deceiving New Age spirits. Since I was a child of God, all that occult activity was confusing, but the slow process of getting biblically educated helped me begin using my gifts for Christ's kingdom, while still loving people from every religion and spiritual practice. My place is not to force change on anyone; I can only love others while speaking the truth I have been shown, planting seeds and then letting the Holy Spirit handle the follow up.

In 2007, as preparation for down the road when my boys would graduate high school, I attended massage therapy school to work in a quiet, peaceful atmosphere away from the rat race, where I could help people to relax and heal their minds, bodies, and spirits. These desires were placed in my heart by God. He made me passionate to help his children through the sort of love, healing, and deliverance talked about in Isaiah 61:1–3:

> *"The Spirit of the Lord God is upon me; because the Lord hath anointed me to preach good tidings unto the meek; he hath sent me to bind up the brokenhearted, to proclaim liberty to the captives, and the opening of the prison to them that are bound; To proclaim the acceptable year of the Lord, and the day of vengeance of our God; to comfort all that mourn; To appoint unto them that mourn in Zion, to give unto them beauty for ashes, the oil of joy for mourning, the garment of praise for the spirit of heaviness; that they might be called trees of righteousness, the planting of the Lord, that he might be glorified."*

But before gaining the biblical wisdom to know exactly who I am in Christ, during my New Age time I failed to recognize the enemy's perversion of my efforts. I was using my free will to journey toward spiritual death. While I desired to help people heal, my lack of biblical knowledge, combined with drug and alcohol use, had me advancing corruption—but could God still use me? Yes! The Lord was allowing me to learn about this quickly advancing false religion (that more and more westerners are getting deceived by today) so that I could better help others caught in it. Now my experience in occult practices keeps me curious about the plight of people God puts in my path, prompting me to see if I can be of assistance. They may not be walking closely with God, which means they are likely being deceived by the enemy in some way, as I was for so long—even as a Christian!

An exciting part of a joyful, Jesus-dedicated life is how God constantly reveals mysteries. Years prior, I attended a school for energy medicine (quantum physics combined with massage), a full on spiritual education in New Age practices. Their techniques had an allure and felt helpful, but never worked for me. I couldn't even participate. My insides—really the Holy Spirit inside me— said, "No!" Since committing to Christ, the Lord has revealed what happened back then: through all my naïve shenanigans and in His infinite grace and mercy, God allowed me to be influenced by corrupting beliefs and practices, but then protected me from those abominations to the Lord. He shielded me from the dark influences of occult methods like energy medicine, tarot-card readings, and speaking to occult spirit guides. Back before I sought God's truth in the Bible—when no one warned me about New Age—the *Holy* Spirit had me leave those experiences with a complete emptiness. First John 4:1-6 cautions and encourages Christians about spiritual matters:

> *"Dear friends, do not believe every spirit, but test the spirits to see whether they are from God, because many false prophets have gone out into the world. This is how you can recognize the Spirit of God: Every spirit that acknowledges that Jesus Christ has come in the flesh is from God, but every spirit that does not acknowledge Jesus is not from God. This is the spirit of the antichrist, which you have heard is coming and even now is already in the world.*
>
> *"You, dear children, are from God and have overcome them, because the one who is in you is greater than the one who is in the world. They are from the world and therefore speak from*

> *the viewpoint of the world, and the world listens to them.*
> *We are from God, and whoever knows God listens to us; but*
> *whoever is not from God does not listen to us. This is how we*
> *recognize the Spirit of truth and the spirit of falsehood."*

While not *of* the New Age world, I dove deep into the occult tools I mentioned, as well as angel cards and worldly self-help books, all focused on *me* and trying to fix *my* life. But instead of continuing that shallow, corrupt, *self*-centered searching, a servant's walk with God and Scripture has taught me so much that helps warn others away from those unfruitful endeavors— and into a relationship with Jesus. The enemy pushes fleeting excitement through all his false faiths, while claiming that Christianity is boring. But Jesus did not come to steal our fun and freedom. Paul said it well in Philippians 1:21:

> *"To live is Christ, and to die is gain."*

Life only becomes truly fulfilling, rewarding, and joyous when you know *who* you are and *Whose* you are—a child of God. But the majority of mankind wrongly decides those eternity changing questions through belief in the claims and experiences of wickedly sinful mankind. Because we live in a fallen world, we never want to rely on the teaching of another person; instead, we only revere Scripture because the evidence is irrefutable that the Bible was given to us by the Holy Spirit, who penned it through men. As God's Word tells us, we were all born with a depraved heart that can only be somewhat tempered through a relationship with Christ (though we still sin during this life):

> *"Scripture indicates that even children have a sin nature,*
> *which argues for the fact that we are born sinners. 'Folly is*
> *bound up in the heart of a child' (Proverbs 22:15). David says,*
> *'Surely I was sinful at birth, / sinful from the time my mother*
> *conceived me' (Psalm 51:5). 'Even from birth the wicked go*
> *astray; / from the womb they are wayward, spreading lies'*
> *(Psalm 58:3).*[6]

Worldly ways almost always harden people against God and His Scriptures, so even professing Christians can end up misinforming, mistreating, and misrepresenting the Lord. This breaks my heart! God offers a relationship; man advocates man's desires. The Lord is appalled at

6 https://www.facebook.com/Restore7/posts/1531395273793974

the world's works-based, Pharisee-type religions, with their hypocritical spirit of following man's ideas instead of God's. Christians can hurt or at least fail to help God's kingdom when they do not keep their eyes solely on Jesus. Try having a spiritual conversation with a supposedly enlightened person. It's so strange. And that makes sense when you read 1 Corinthians 2:14–16, where the Apostle Paul wrote about these kinds of interactions (near the end he tucks Isaiah 40:13 into his comments):

> "The person **without** the Spirit does not accept the things that come from the Spirit of God but considers them foolishness, and cannot understand them because they are discerned only through the Spirit. The person **with** the Spirit makes judgments about all things, but such a person is not subject to merely human judgments, for, 'Who has known the mind of the Lord so as to instruct him?' But we have the mind of Christ."

The fact that believers have the mind of Jesus is not meant as a boast, but to help others understand that the spiritual maturity of Christ followers is exponentially—divinely—superior to any other spirituality. In fact, *every* unbiblical belief and practice is not eternal; those falsities are superficial and temporary to this life, like New Age philosophies that teach "connectedness" with the universe, instead of an everlasting relationship with the Creator of it (space is just created matter with no power or consciousness). The westernized Hinduism and Buddhism of the New Age movement are forms of spiritualism that attempt to counterfeit the power of the Holy Spirit.

Hindus and their modern New Age followers invite the Kundalini spirit (a demonic entity) to spiritually connect with them through yoga, meditation, chants, reiki, and Taoism, or even while being intimate with an already possessed person. Again, these sorts of beliefs and practices attempt to yoke the participant with spirits that are not from God. Here is an excellent explanation of the New Age movement from Pastor Billy Crone, a formerly demon-possessed New Ager who was radically saved one Easter morning when he called on Jesus:

> "It was a big part of my life before getting saved. The philosophy teaches that anything goes. An adherent can create his or her own right and wrong, which of course is a lie. New Age is the combination of a great many practices—with a lot of dark stuff mixed in—and can get evil very quickly. It's

a westernized blend of many ancient and modern Hindu and Buddhist religions and philosophies combined with occult practices.

"Eastern religions have been 'evangelizing' America for decades with messages in our movies, games, schools, yoga, meditation, and everywhere else they can. But it's just the same old lie from Satan that he tricked Eve with in the Garden of Eden, which is that you or I can be God, deciding for ourselves what is right and wrong, good and evil. Anything goes. For me as a young person searching for life's purpose, it was appealing because young and rebellious people everywhere tend to reject having to listen and submit to anyone, including God.

"Especially youth, but people of all ages are vulnerable to the New Age message that falsely promises they can make up their own truth, morality, and eternity. As one guy said, it preaches political correctness, which claims, 'MY truth over THE truth.' But THE truth from God involves consequences that have to do with where they WILL spend eternity, and GOD will decide that."[7]

Without biblical knowledge, vast portions of mankind are easily sucked in by these deceptions. And I understand why: New Age allowed me to appear open-minded and offered almost any idea from man— except salvation through Christ *alone*. In fact, over the past 2000 years, many cults and other pagan practices have included Christian Scripture and Christian-sounding language ("Christianese") in an attempt to also capture believers' lives, leading them to neglect the purpose Jesus has for them. New Age is like a buffet of beliefs and practices, where *you* get to decide what *your* truth is. Believing in a little bit of everything made me feel accepting, loving, and tolerant. I certainly did not want to seem religious! I was on the broad path that believes lies instead of the truth, which is that we need the Savior to fill the God-sized hole in our souls. Like many, I believed in Jesus, celebrated Christmas and Easter, and even professed Jesus as my personal Lord and Savior (all through the drinking and New Age spiritual practices), but my heart was far from Christ, so I had no personal relationship with Him.

7 From Day 173 of the book *Wisdom in a Year: 365 Days of Questions & Answers That Will Change Your Life* by Pastor Billy Crone of Sunrise Bible Church (Las Vegas, NV) and *GetALifeMedia.com* (probable publication late 2022)

The most important decision in this life will be whether you believe Jesus is the *only* way to God. Some say He was just a great philosopher, prophet, or teacher, but irrefutable evidence from multiple Jewish, Christian, and even secular sources show that Jesus was more than just a great man—He was also God (fully man *and* fully God). And if you are going to believe what He said, you must trust Christ when He claimed over and over that He was God manifested on earth and is still God. Either He is who He says He is, or He is a complete liar. In John 14:6 Jesus declared:

> *"I am the way and the truth and the life.* ***No one*** *comes to the Father except through me."*

The Bible says you and I serve either our Heavenly Father or the enemy. There is no in-between. Every human has been made in God's image, meaning you are immortal, and the Lord gave you the freedom to serve who you would like in this life. But who you serve at your last breath is the good or evil entity you will serve for eternity—meaning it is the most consequential decision of your life on earth. Who do you want to spend eternity with?

I choose to believe Jesus, who told us that the Father and He are one. Therefore, contrary to the teachings of New Age, every path does not lead to an inconsequential or heavenly end. The enemy has created a multitude of alternatives that you can choose in your rejection of Christ but taking yourself away from Jesus leads to your decision of a horrific eternity separated from Him. Instead, my plumb line is to always heed the warning in 2 Peter 2:1-3:

> *"But there were also false prophets among the people, just as there will be false teachers among you. They will secretly introduce destructive heresies, even denying the sovereign Lord who bought them—bringing swift destruction on themselves. Many will follow their depraved conduct and will bring the way of truth into disrepute. In their greed these teachers will exploit you with fabricated stories. Their condemnation has long been hanging over them, and their destruction has not been sleeping."*

We must not fall for the philosophies of men—eternity is forever! Do your beliefs come from your own careful research, or are you taking someone's word for the truth? Do you feel your beliefs are true, or are your views based on facts? There is overwhelming, undeniable proof that our Bible is the Word of God, written by the Holy Spirit through men. That evidence is available for all those who care enough to seek it out. Again, eternity is forever. I waited decades to do the research myself, wasting so many years before finally coming to the entire truth of Scripture.

Crystals are still beautiful, I feel closer to God when in nature, I love relaxation and massage, and I prefer the organic and holistic lifestyle. I think those things are part of the way we're meant to live but experiencing them in close relationship with God makes all the difference. With Him I became free to belong (to Him and the Christian family), find my career and purpose, get the education I desired (it turned out to be Christian ministry), find the relationships I longed for (heavenly and earthly), and use the gifts God clearly gave me to edify and build up my children (and many of His). That God-sized hole in my heart was finally filled, and I am now walking with Jesus—Who I love and adore—in true fulfillment of my purpose, knowing the difference between deceptive self-focused religion, and love of and sacrifice for others. Those who never pick up a Bible will miss the understanding of many mysteries, spiritual experiences with your Creator who speaks of true and pure love, like we hear about in 1 John 4:7–18:

> "Dear friends, let us love one another, for love comes from God. Everyone who loves has been born of God and knows God. Whoever does not love does not know God, because God is love. This is how God showed his love among us: He sent his one and only Son into the world that we might live through him. This is love: not that we loved God, but that he loved us and sent his Son as an atoning sacrifice for our sins. Dear friends, since God so loved us, we also ought to love one another. No one has ever seen God; but if we love one another, God lives in us and his love is made complete in us.

> "This is how we know that we live in him and he in us: He has given us of his Spirit. And we have seen and testify that the Father has sent his Son to be the Savior of the world. If anyone acknowledges that Jesus is the Son of God, God lives in them and they in God. And so we know and rely on the love God has for us. God is love. Whoever lives in love lives in God, and God in them. This is how love is made complete among us so that we will have confidence on the Day of Judgment: In this world we are like Jesus. There is no fear in love. But perfect love drives out fear, because fear has to do with punishment. The one who fears is not made perfect in love."

That passage mentions how God sends the Holy Spirit to live inside every Christian. I have been fortunate to learn the gifts of the Spirit, who helps us fight for the faith and accomplish Jesus-like signs, miracles, and wonders. Yet the vast majority of people—including believers—do not know of or understand who the Holy Spirit is, an unfathomably wonderful gift given by God to help us navigate this world. Jesus explains the Holy Spirit in John 16:7 and 14:15–17:

> *"But very truly I tell you, it is for your good that I am going away. Unless I go away, the Advocate [Holy Spirit] will not come to you; but if I go, I will send him to you."*

> *"If you love me, keep my commands. And I will ask the Father, and he will give you another advocate to help you and be with you forever—the Spirit of truth. The world cannot accept him, because it neither sees him nor knows him. But you know him, for he lives with you and will be in you."*

Addendum 2
End-Times Bible Prophecy

Much of the following end-days information is from Pastor Billy Crone at *GetALifeMedia.com,* and the chart is from Bill Salus with *ProphecyDepotMinistries.net.* Also, we highly recommend subscribing to *EndTimes.com,* which is from Pastor Jimmy Evans' *Tipping Point Prophecies.* Pastor Billy Crone has appeared several times on his platform. All three wonderful warriors for Jesus are strictly biblical, Christian brothers. Pastor Billy has excellent documentaries on the Christian rapture and Revelation's seal judgements. Bill Salus wrote the easy-reference set of end-times books that you see on the chart below.[8] [9] [10] Also look for Jimmy Evans' book *Where Are the Missing People?,* which would be great for every Christian to leave behind on their kitchen tables—for those who will want to know where believers have gone after the rapture of Christ's Church.

8 https://vimeo.com/ondemand/therapturedontbedeceived
9 https://vimeo.com/ondemand/theseals
10 http://www.prophecydepotministries.net

When the rapture suddenly happens without warning, in the "twinkling of an eye," the nonChristians left behind on earth will go through the calm of a deceptive peace agreement that will be signed by the Antichrist, Israel, and some other party not identified in Scripture. That begins the seven-year tribulation, a time kicked off with the "seal judgments." These include the four horsemen of the Apocalypse bringing the wrath of God through global war, famine, and plagues, along with death to a quarter of mankind. After three and a half years of the four horsemen and that false treaty, the Satan-led Antichrist will reveal his evil intentions when he goes into the rebuilt Jewish temple, sits on the Lord's throne, and proclaims himself to be God.

That begins the second half of the seven-year tribulation, called the Great Tribulation. God continues pouring out His wrath on an unrepentant mankind, as the Antichrist massacres two thirds of the Jewish people (God protects a third), while Jews and the rest of mankind go through the worst time of death and destruction in earth's history, as Jesus tells us in Matthew 24:21–22:

> "For at that time there will be great tribulation, unmatched from the beginning of the world until now, and never to be seen again. If those days had not been cut short, no one would survive, but for the sake of the elect those days will be shortened."

God's wrath continues with a global earthquake, the sun turning black and the moon red (a blood moon), asteroids hitting all over the world, mountains and islands removed—and then come the "trumpet judgments." Those start with silence in heaven, followed by fiery hail raining down to burn up a third of the earth, a huge asteroid that kills a third of the sea and destroys the same amount the ships, and a blazing comet that strikes, causing much death from a third of the rivers and fresh water turning bitter. Then one-third of the sun, moon, and stars are struck, causing a third of the day and night to be without light, followed by Satan releasing a demon horde of locusts to spend five months torturing those who took the mark of the beast. Then four fallen angels are loosed from under the Euphrates River to kill a third of mankind.

Next are the "bowl judgments" with painful sores appearing on those who took the mark of the beast, and all sea creatures die when the seas turn to blood, as do all rivers and fresh water. The sun scorches people with fire—yet they still curse God—the kingdom of the Antichrist is plunged into darkness, the Euphrates River dries up, and three evil frog spirits—along with Satan, the Antichrist, and the False (religious) Prophet—deceive the world into thinking they can defeat Jesus when He returns—spoiler, they don't. Then comes the greatest of all earthquakes that hits the whole earth, Jerusalem is split in three, all the world's cities collapse, all islands and mountains are gone, and a massive storm hits with 100-pound hail stones. Then comes the Battle of Armageddon where Christ returns at His second coming and defeats His enemies (their blood runs four feet deep for two hundred miles). Next, God's angels harvest the righteous and unrighteous, throwing the latter into the lake of fire.

Unrepentant masses have hardened hearts during the tribulation, but some accept Jesus because their family or friends were raptured, the newly saved will save others, God's angels proclaim Christ around the earth, there is a group of 144,000 Jews who witness for Jesus, and the two witnesses in Jerusalem will also share the gospel worldwide—probably from being filmed— before the Antichrist finally kills them during the Great Tribulation. So, people can be saved after the rapture but they will go through the seven-year tribulation. Most will be viciously martyred for their faith.

During this hellish time on our planet, Christ will have taken His bride (the Christians He met in the air) back to heaven for the marriage supper of the lamb (our Savior Jesus), a celebration that will last many years while God pours out His wrath on the left-behind, unrepentant, wickedly sinful unbelievers. At the end of that celebration in heaven, all God's children will follow Jesus back to earth, where He will vanquish the last forces of evil and set up His millennial kingdom for earth's last thousand years. That will make a tidy *seven thousand years*, which parallels the *seventh day* God rested after making all creation.

That last millennium will have Jesus running the world from Jerusalem, with believers ruling and reigning alongside Him, at levels commensurate with how much of their lives were spent contributing to the advancement of God's kingdom: those who did more will be given more to rule over. That final thousand years will include the human offspring of believers who survived the seven-year tribulation. They will not have glorified bodies. But like Jesus, raptured Christians (who attended the marriage supper of the lamb and then came back to earth with Him) will rule and reign in their glorified, sinless bodies—praise God!

After that last thousand years (of seven thousand total for mankind), the Lord will create a whole new heavens and earth called the Eternal State—with no sin! That end of the old, sinful earth will bring us full circle back to why the Lord originally made humans and did so in His image: God is love, and love loves to love. He wanted more beings to love, to share His love with.

But God cannot be around freewill humans who chose to sin. The body of a sinful person would be obliterated in the full presence of our all-powerful, sinless Creator. To survive communing with (living with and fully embracing) God, a sinful person must be pardoned for their sins by accepting the Messiah's (Jesus's, or the Lamb or God's) sacrifice for forgiveness of their sins. If so, their sins are eradicated in the Lord's eyes, meaning He can commune with them as He did in the Garden of Eden with Adam and Eve before they sinned. He created them as sinless people, put them in a perfect Garden of Eden, and gave them dominion over the earth. But when they followed the sinful ways that Satan invented, it all became fallen, and the devil got dominion of what had been mankind's. However, those original sinless conditions will again be seen with the new heavens and earth, a universal Garden of Eden where we are in incorruptible, glorified bodies, meaning we can commune with our Heavenly Father.

All God's will for an eternal future that will involve communing with mankind is going to be done, despite us using the freewill He gave us to initially mess it all up for thousands of years (an insignificant amount of time compared to eternity). Sadly, many do not choose to follow God, so they sit in their sins and the Lord cannot live with sin. If only they would choose God by accepting Jesus's sacrifice to cover their sins, they too would have the amazing future we Christians are looking forward to—praise God! Again, as Paul says, "to live is Christ and to die is gain." It sure is! Amen!

www.ingramcontent.com/pod-product-compliance
Lightning Source LLC
Chambersburg PA
CBHW070658130626
46553CB00005B/1756